GOD SOVEREIGN

AND

MAN FREE:

OR THE DOCTRINE OF

DIVINE FOREORDINATION

AND

MAN'S FREE AGENCY,

STATED, ILLUSTRATED AND PROVED FROM THE SCRIPTURES.

By N. L. RICE, D.D.

PHILADELPHIA:
PRESBYTERIAN BOARD OF PUBLICATION,
No. 1334 CHESTNUT STREET.

PREFACE.

HAPPY would it be for the Church of Christ and for the world, if Christian ministers and Christian people could be contented to be *disciples*,—LEARNERS; if, conscious of their limited faculties, their ignorance of divine things, and their proneness to err through depravity and prejudice, they could be induced to sit at the feet of Jesus and learn of him. The Church has been corrupted and cursed in almost every age by the undue confidence of men in their reasoning powers. They have undertaken to pronounce upon the reasonableness or unreasonableness of doctrines infinitely above their reason, which are necessarily matters of pure revelation. In their presumption they have sought to comprehend "the deep things of God," and have interpreted the Scriptures, not according to their obvious meaning, but according to the decisions of their finite reason.

On no subject have men affirmed and denied more boldly, than that of *Divine foreordination.* Had the question been, as it ought to have been, simply concerning the obvious teaching of the Scriptures,—had men been content to interpret the language of Inspiration according to the acknowledged principles of interpretation, the faith of Christians might have been far more harmonious. But before turning to the word of God, they have filled their minds with objections; and then they have exhausted their learning in attempting so to interpret the language of Scripture, as to avoid the difficulties they saw in its obvious meaning.—Strange that they who object to this mode of proceeding concerning the doctrine of the Trinity, should yet resort to it in determining the truth of the doctrine of Divine foreordination. For if we cannot comprehend the mode of God's existence, because it is infinitely above us, for the same reason we cannot comprehend the counsels of infinite wisdom. No one has ever studied the works of Nature or the Book of Revelation without finding himself encompassed on every side by difficulties he could not solve. The philosopher is obliged to be satisfied with *facts;* and the theologian must content himself with God's declarations. The philosopher must not reject facts, because he cannot reconcile them with the perfections of God or the accountability of man; and the theologian must believe the plain teaching of God's word, though he cannot solve the difficulties which seem to him to press upon it.

It is necessary that the doctrine of Divine foreordination be frequently discussed, not only because it has important practical bearings, but because it has been and is more misrepresented and caricatured than almost any other doctrine of the Scriptures. The doctrines of Christianity are not mere abstractions, but great practical truths, designed and adapted, through the influence of the Holy Spirit, to mould the affections of the heart and to give a right direction to the conduct. Both the advocates and the opponents of the doctrine of Divine decrees agree in attributing to it most important practical tendencies. If the doctrine is true, those tendencies must be good; if false, we will acknowledge them to be evil. The subject, then, demands a fair and candid investigation. And if we do not greatly err, those who give it such an investigation, will find the doctrine abundantly sustained by the Scriptures, and not pressed with any difficulty which should weaken our faith in it. Nay, they will see, that they must receive it; or, if consistent in rejecting it, they must reject some of the fundamental doctrines of Christianity.

The following volume is designed clearly to state the doctrine, as held by Calvinists, and to prove it true both by *its fruits* and by *the direct testimony of God's word.* The first chapter exhibits very briefly the fruits of Calvinism, where it is admitted to have prevailed; and in the following chapters the doctrine of Divine foreordination, in its two great branches, is clearly stated and defended. The author, however, has not been disposed to act simply on the defensive. He has deemed it proper to enter into a careful examination of some of the most serious errors of the opposite system. Without entertaining any other than the kindest feelings toward those who differ from him, he has felt at liberty,—rather he has deemed it his duty,—freely to examine the claims of some of their doctrines.

It is possible that the methods of stating and illustrating this important doctrine, adopted by the author, may strike forcibly the minds of some, and assist them in rightly understanding it. If so, he will not have labored in vain. With a sincere desire to contribute somewhat to the spread of sound doctrine, and thus to promote the glory of the Redeemer and the eternal happiness of men, he ventures, with prayer for the Divine blessing upon it, to throw before the Christian public this volume. Should it be lost amid the multitude of abler works, he will not be disposed to complain, but will rather rejoice, that the cause of truth and righteousness has many advocates more competent than himself.

CONTENTS.

PART I.

DIVINE FOREORDINATION.

PART II.

DOCTRINE OF ELECTION.

CHAPTER I.

CHAPTER II.

CHAPTER III.

CHAPTER IV.

CHAPTER V.

CHAPTER VI.

GOD SOVEREIGN AND MAN FREE.

PART I.

CHAPTER I.

THE DOCTRINE OF DIVINE FOREORDINATION PROVED TO BE SCRIPTURAL BY ITS FRUITS.

HAS God from eternity foreordained whatsoever comes to pass? If he has, how is this doctrine consistent with the free agency and accountability of angels and men, and with the Divine perfections? These are important questions, which, in the fear of God, and guided by his word, we propose briefly to examine.

As represented by many of its opponents, the doctrine of Divine foreordination is, we admit, unscriptural, absurd and impious. It is represented as making God the efficient author of all the moral feelings and acts of his rational creatures, as thus destroying their free agency, and as striking at the very foundations of morality. Are these representations of the doctrine correct? There are two ways of obtaining a satisfactory answer to this question, viz: first, by inquiring what have been the *fruits* of this and its kindred doctrines, where they have prevailed; and, secondly, by distinctly stating the doctrine, and comparing it with the teachings of the word of God. We propose briefly to adopt both these methods.

First. What have been the *fruits* of the doctrine of

Divine foreordination, where it has prevailed? This doctrine, let it be observed, stands not alone, but is an *essential part* of a system of doctrines which has been called Calvinistic, in distinction from a different system called Arminian. Now the principle is admitted by all Christians, that there is an inseparable connection between religious truth and sound morality,—that the uniform effect of Scriptural truth, wherever it is sincerely embraced, is to lead to virtuous feelings and conduct. It is admitted, also, that the moral tendencies of religious error upon the character and conduct of men, are decidedly bad, and bad precisely in proportion to the greatness of the error. To the Jews, who, blinded by religious error, had become slaves of sin, our Saviour said, "Ye shall know the truth, and the truth shall make you free."* And the inspired Paul triumphantly appealed to the fruits of his doctrines, as exhibited in the lives of his converts, as the best evidence that they were from God. "Do we begin again to commend ourselves? or need we, as some others, epistles of commendation to you, or letters of commendation from you? Ye are our epistle written in our hearts, known and read of all men: forasmuch as ye are manifestly declared to be the epistle of Christ ministered by us, written not with ink, but with the Spirit of the living God; not in tables of stone, but in fleshly tables of the heart."† The reflecting mind needs no more conclusive evidence of the falsity of the various systems of Paganism, of Deism, of Mahometanism, and of Popery, than that afforded by their corrupt fruits. Their effects upon the moral character of their zealous

* John 8: 32. † 2 Corinthians 3: 1–3,

defenders, and upon the character of the communities where they have respectively prevailed, have ever been held up by Christians in contrast with the moral effects of Christianity, as conclusive evidence of the truth of the latter. We are prepared to try Calvinism, as it is called, by this admitted principle. If it is what its opposers represent it, its effects upon the morals of those who have held and do hold it, must have been extremely bad. John Wesley said, that it makes "all preaching vain;" that "it directly tends to destroy that holiness, which is the end of all the ordinances of God;" that it "directly tends to destroy our zeal for good works;" that it has "also a direct and manifest tendency to overthrow the whole Christian revelation;" that it represents our Saviour "as a hypocrite, a deceiver of the people, a man void of common sincerity;" that it "destroys all God's attributes at once: it overturns both his justice, mercy and truth: yea, it represents the most holy God as worse than the devil, as both more false, more cruel and more unjust," as "an omnipresent, almighty tyrant." "This," says he, "is the blasphemy clearly contained in the *horrible decree* of predestination."* This is a tolerably full epitome of the charges alleged against the doctrine of Divine foreordination. What must inevitably be the effects of a system of doctrine, of which this constitutes one of the most prominent features, upon the moral character of those who embrace it, and of those communities where it prevails? Immorality, of course, in its various forms must prevail; good works must be wholly disregarded; infidelity must abound; and the people, like the Being

* Sermon on Free Grace.

whom they worship, must become as bad, as unjust, as cruel, as the devil, and even more so!

Now let us turn from this picture, and inquire what have been the real fruits of Calvinism in all countries and in all ages.

It will not be denied, that Augustine, bishop of Hippo, who lived in the latter part of the fourth and in the beginning of the fifth centuries, held the doctrine of Divine foreordination, and its kindred doctrines, now called Calvinistic. That he was an eminently good, as well as great man, and that his labors and writings, more than those of any other man in the age in which he lived, contributed to the promotion of sound doctrine and the revival of true religion, no candid man, acquainted with the history of the Church, will deny. In his day the Pelagian heresy arose, and threatened to spread its withering influence over the Church; "and to him indeed," as the historian Mosheim says, "is principally due the glory of having suppressed this sect in its very birth." It was in the midst of this controversy, as the same historian states, that Augustine delivered his views concerning "the necessity of divine grace in order to our salvation, and the decrees of God with respect to the future condition of men;" and when certain Monks advanced the doctrine so often charged upon Calvinists, "that God not only predestinated the wicked to eternal punishment, but also to the guilt and transgression for which they were punished; and that thus both the good and the bad actions of all men were determined from eternity, and fixed by an invincible necessity;" Augustine made as decided opposition to this doctrine, as to Pelagianism, "and explained his true sentiments with more perspicuity, that it might not be attributed to him."*

Amongst the earlier believers in the system of doctrine called Calvinistic, we may, with great propriety, mention the Waldenses and Albigenses,—those eminent and honored witnesses for the truth, during the long period when the Church and the world were overrun with gross error and immorality. In one of their Creeds, containing a brief summary of their faith, "which," say they, "hath been taught them from the father to the sonne for these many hundred yeares, and taken out of the word of God," the second Article is as follows: "All that have been, or shall be saved, have been chosen of God before all worlds." The fourth Article reads thus: "Whosoever holdeth free-will [i. e., in the Pelagian sense], denieth wholly the predestination of God."† It is difficult with certainty to trace this wonderful people to their origin; but certain it is, that no body of people under the sun have so long and so firmly held an evangelical faith and a sound morality, against the most protracted and cruel persecutions. All evangelical Protestants look to them as the heroic defenders of the faith once delivered to the saints, during long ages of universal corruption. And when the glorious Reformation of the sixteenth century commenced, "these scattered adherents to the faith once delivered to the saints," as Dr. Fisk, an eminent Methodist writer, remarks, "were prepared to give aid and influence to the first general struggle that was made to reform the impurities of the Church."‡

---

* Vol. 1, pt. 2, p. 372.

† See Perrin's History.

‡ Fisk's Travels, p. 122.

The Reformation was a glorious event. The Christian world regard it as a wonderful revival of true religion, wrought by the Spirit of God,—as the dawn of a brighter day in the history of the Church, and in the history of civil and religious liberty. And who were the men chosen of God to be the instruments in accomplishing this mighty work, in elevating once more the cross of Christ, and in staying the overwhelming tide of tyranny, superstition and immorality? They were men who held and preached the Calvinistic doctrines. For, although the doctrine of Divine foreordination and its kindred doctrines have been called by the name of John Calvin, their most illustrious defender, it is well known, that the other reformers, Luther, Melancthon, Zuinglius, Œcolampadius, Knox and Cranmer, all held the same views; and hence all the creeds drawn up by those men of God are decidedly Calvinistic.

It is truly an instructive fact, that when error and superstition were rapidly overruning the Church in the close of the fourth and in the beginning of the fifth century, the most effective opposition was made by an eminent minister holding the views afterward so successfully defended by Calvin and the reformers. It is a fact no less instructive, that during the dark ages, sound doctrine and pure morality found a retreat in the fastnesses of the Alps, and were wonderfully defended and preserved by the Calvinistic Waldenses and Albigenses. It is a fact which speaks volumes for Calvinism, that the most glorious revolution recorded in the history of the church and of the world, since the days of the Apostles, was effected by the blessing of God upon its doctrines. Whatever there is of evangelical doctrine, and of civil and religious liberty in the world, must be traced, under God, to the writings and the preaching of Calvinists.

The thirty-nine Articles of the church of England are decidedly Calvinistic; and in the days of her greatest purity her Ministry preached most faithfully the doctrines of her Creed. On the other hand, as her vital piety and spirituality declined, and her morality became more and more lax, this favorable change was marked by a change as decided from Calvinistic to Arminian sentiments. About the time when the notorious Archbishop Laud flourished, Macaulay says,—"A divine of that age, who was asked by a simple country gentleman what the Arminians held, answered, with as much truth as wit, that they held all the best Bishoprics and Deaneries of England."* Laud and his Clergy were most zealously Arminian in their theology, and at the same time they displayed a spirit of bigotry and persecution which was scarcely exceeded by Rome herself; and the corruption of their morals was equaled only by their zeal for Arminian doctrines. But in every age, the most evangelical and spiritual Ministers of the Church of England, have been decided Calvinists; and those of an opposite character have been decided Arminians. Dr. Thomas Scott, the celebrated Commentator, while an unconverted Minister of that Church, was an Arian, and a bitter opposer of the Calvinistic doctrines. When truly converted, he not only renounced Arianism, but became a firm and consistent Calvinist; and from that day he was an eminently good and useful man. He was confirmed, as he states, in the belief of the Calvinistic doctrines, by the fact, "that

* Macaulay's History, vol. 1, p. 74.

they were admitted, at the beginning of the reformation, into the creeds, catechisms, or articles of every one of the Protestant churches; that our [Episcopal], articles and homilies expressly maintained them: and, consequently, that a vast number of wise and sober-minded men, who, in their days, were burning and shining lights, upon mature deliberation, had agreed, not only that they were true, but that they ought to be admitted as useful, or even as necessary articles of faith by every one, who deemed himself called to take upon him the office of a Christian minister."* Legh Richmond, whose praise will long be in all the churches, was a Calvinist. But we need not mention particular names. Go and inquire into the theology of the High-church-men and Puseyites of England and America, and you will find not a Calvinist among them. Then inquire into that of the most evangelical of the Low Church ministers, and you will find among them few, if any, Arminians.

For three centuries past, the character of the Scotch has been moulded by a strictly Calvinistic theology. And what country on the globe has exhibited a purer morality? What church has embraced a greater number of eminently pious people, or can exhibit a larger list of martyrs for the cause of Christ? What Church has made so firm and uncompromising opposition to tyranny, and done so much for civil and religious liberty? And where is there now a Church of such liberality in giving to the cause of Christ, or doing more for the spread of the Gospel, than the Free Church of Scotland? In that

* Force of Truth.

Church, freed from the trammels of civil interference, Calvinism is now exhibiting its real character, and bringing forth its legitimate fruits.

Nor do we hesitate to point the opposers of Calvinism to the Presbyterian church of these United States, to all the different branches of the Presbyterian church in Europe and America, and to the Puritans of Old England and of New England, and to challenge a comparison of their morals, their good works, their efforts to promote the spread of the gospel, their labors in the cause of liberty and of education, with any other denomination or class of denominations holding Arminian sentiments. Even in the victorious army of Oliver Cromwell, a purity of morals unknown in military bodies, was preserved. "But that which chiefly distinguished the army of Cromwell from other armies," says Macaulay, "was the austere morality and the fear of God which pervaded all ranks. It is acknowledged by the most zealous royalists that, in that singular camp, no oath was heard, no drunkenness or gambling was seen, and that, during the long dominion of the soldiery, the property of the peaceable citizen and the honor of woman were held sacred. If outrages were committed, they were outrages of a very different kind from those of which a victorious army is generally guilty. No servant-girl complained of the rough gallantry of the red coats; not an ounce of plate was taken from the shops of the goldsmiths," etc.* That Puritan army were not faultless; far from it; but we may safely challenge the opposers of Calvinism to produce another in the records of history of as pure morality.

---

* Macaulay's History, vol. 1, p. 114.

There is another fact illustrative of the true character of the Calvinistic doctrines, which we must not pass unnoticed, viz: *that those doctrines have never been found associated with fundamental error.* The history of the Christian church affords not an instance of a sect holding the doctrines of *Divine Decrees and Man's Free Agency,* and rejecting any doctrine which is fundamental to Christianity. Some heretics have held the doctrine of Divine Decrees, and denied Man's Free Agency; and some have held the latter and denied the former; but no heretical sect was ever known to hold both Divine Decrees and Free Agency as these doctrines are held by Calvinists. On the contrary, if any man or class of men professing to be Calvinists, have abandoned the fundamental doctrines of Christianity, they have commenced their downward course by renouncing the doctrines peculiar to Calvinism. The celebrated Dr. Priestly commenced his wanderings by becoming an Arminian, and ended them by embracing a Materialistic Universalism. Out of a multitude of examples which might be given, we select one. In the progress of the great revival which spread rapidly over the Western States, in the beginning of the present century, several Presbyterian ministers of some prominence, left the church, and fell into fatal errors. Of these, some united with the Shakers; one became the father of a new Arian sect, called NEW-LIGHTS; and two returned to the church. Among the firsts acts of these men, after leaving the church, was the publication of an "Apology," in which they denied "the positions of the Confession of Faith in regard to the Divine Decrees, the Atonement, and the special influences of the Spirit in the production of faith."* Never was it known, that any man holding the doctrine of Divine Decrees and Free Agency, embraced fundamental error, without renouncing this doctrine.

Now if the Calvinistic doctrines are of the demoralizing, God-dishonoring character charged by their opponents, how shall we account, in the first place, for their effects upon the moral character of men; and, in the second, for their entire separation, at all times, from all fundamental errors?

1. How shall we account for their *fruits*, or effects upon moral character? They are said to destroy the truth of revelation; and yet those holding them have stood in the front ranks of the defenders of revelation; and no communities have been more free from skepticism, than those among whom these doctrines have been most faithfully preached. They are said to be irreconcilable with human accountability, and thus to destroy the very foundations of morals; and yet no people on earth have manifested a deeper and more abiding sense of their accountability, or maintained a purer morality, than Calvinists. In this respect even their enemies have been constrained to bear a strong testimony in their favor. The Calvinistic doctrines are said to be decidedly unfavorable to good works; and yet no denomination of Christians on earth have manifested a greater zeal for good works, or have endured more self-denial in performing them, than those whose faith is Calvinistic. They are said to make preaching useless, and to quiet the con-

* Davidson's History of the Presbyterian Church in Kentucky, p. 195.

sciences of sinners; and yet no class of ministers in the world have preached with more zeal or with more powerful effects, than those holding and preaching these doctrines. Think of the incessant labors of such men as David Brainerd, Henry Martyn, and a multitude like them, for the conversion of the heathen. And then compare the preaching of such men as George Whitfield, Rowland Hill, Richard Baxter, Legh Richmond, President Edwards, Samuel Davies, William Tennant, Dr. Nettleton, and a multitude of others, with that of any similar number of Arminian preachers the world ever produced, and we fear not the verdict of the impartial. The Calvinistic doctrines are said to be very unfavorable to high attainments in piety; and yet a larger proportion of persons eminently pious, and of books calculated to promote spirituality, cannot be found, than the Calvinistic churches present. Read Doddridge's Rise and Progress of Religion in the Soul, Owen on the Spirit, Baxter's Saint's Everlasting Rest, Bunyan's Pilgrim, John Newton's works, Legh Richmond's Dairyman's Daughter, Guthrie's Christian's Great Interest, Alexander's Religious Experience, Edwards on the Affections, the Biographies of Martyn, Payson, Brainerd, etc., etc.

Now how are we to account for the clear and certain fact, that the *effects* of the Calvinistic doctrines have been not only widely different from their alleged tendencies, but diametrically opposite to them? How has it happened, if their decided tendency is to produce certain evil effects, that the effects actually produced have been of an entirely opposite character? The opponents of these doctrines must take one of the following positions: First, that the facts stated concerning the moral character of Calvinists, are not true; or, second, that they have not really believed the doctrines taught in their creeds, catechisms, and theological books; or, third, that they hold so much truth as to neutralize the effects of their errors; or, fourth, that blasphemous error may produce as sound morality as truth; or, fifth, that the Calvinistic doctrines are scriptural and true.

Will they deny the facts stated concerning the moral and religious character of Calvinists? They cannot; for faithful history, not written by Calvinists, has recorded the past, and the present speaks for itself. We point to the Calvinistic denominations of the present day, and say; behold the fruits of Calvinism!

Will the opponents of Calvinism deny, that Calvinists have really held the doctrines of their creed? Surely it will be admitted, that they know what they believe. It would be strange, indeed, if they did not believe them, since they are impressed upon their minds from the days of childhood. Who does not know, that the great mass of the children of Scotland, for long generations, have been thoroughly drilled in the Shorter Catechism from infancy? And who does not know, that in this country, that catechism is to be found in the great majority of the families and in the Sabbath-schools of Presbyterians and Congregationalists? Beside, the Calvinistic doctrines are preached in all our pulpits, and defended in all our religious papers, from week to week, and from year to year.

Will it be said, that Calvinists hold so much truth, that their errors are neutralized, and therefore produce little or no injurious effects? This will not be pretended;

for the opponents of Calvinism do roundly affirm, that these doctrines neutralize or destroy all others; that they subvert man's free agency and accountability; that they discourage the performance of good works; that they destroy the very foundations of morality. Beside, these doctrines have always been very prominent in the Calvinistic system, and have ever given character to it. It is impossible, therefore, that their deleterious effects, if they tended to produce such, should not have become perfectly manifest long ago. Will it be said, that blasphemous error, though it tends to immorality, may yet produce, for centuries together, pure morality and an abundance of good works? No sane man will maintain a position so absurd. The conclusion, then, appears inevitable, that the Calvinistic doctrines, if judged by their fruits (and there is no safer way of judging), are scriptural and true.

2. And how shall we account for the indubitable fact, that these doctrines have always been associated with the great doctrines of the cross? False doctrines, it is admitted, are often associated with the true, but more frequently they will be found with the false; just as a bad man may sometimes be found in good company, but will generally seek that which is more congenial to his feelings. But the man who always chooses the company of the good, and who is most disliked by the vicious, must be a good man. It is certainly a very remarkable fact, that the doctrines of Divine Foreordination and Free Agency have never, in a single instance, been associated with heresy in any of its forms. If they were of the world, would not the world love its own? If they were

of the devil, would not some of his children admire and embrace them? If they afforded the best excuse for sin, would they not be most agreeable to sinners? We leave the oppoṣers of these doctrines to answer these questions, while we proceed to state and defend, from the direct testimony of God's word, the doctrine of **Divine Decrees.**

CHAPTER II.

THE DOCTRINE OF DIVINE FOREORDINATION STATED, AND THE STATEMENT SHOWN TO BE IN ACCORDANCE WITH THE SCRIPTURES, THE WESTMINSTER CONFESSION OF FAITH AND WITH STANDARD CALVINISTIC WRITERS.

THE purposes of God relate to the *creation* and the *government* of all things.

1. God created all things. This truth no Christian disputes; nor will any one pretend, that the work of creation was an *accidental* work. All will readily admit, that God first formed the purpose to create, and then put forth the creative act in fulfillment of that purpose. All Christians will adopt the language of the Psalmist,—"O Lord, how manifold are thy works! In wisdom hast thou made them all." All unite in saying,—"The heavens declare the glory of God,"—the glory of his wisdom, power, and benevolence.

2. But God purposed to *govern* the world which he created. No Christian believes, that the creation of this world was *the end* of God's purposes concerning it,—that he determined to create the world and place man in it, and then to leave both the world and man to their fortunes. All must agree (for the Scriptures abundantly declare it), that in creating the world he had in view some great end or ends worthy of his infinite perfections; and that he is now governing the world so as to accomplish those ends.

Of the purposes of God concerning the affairs of this world, we read in such passages of Scripture as the following: "I am God, and there is none like me, declaring the end from the beginning, and from ancient times the things that are not yet done, saying, My counsel shall stand, and I will do all my pleasure."* Again,—"The Lord bringeth the counsel of the heathen to naught: he maketh the devices of the people of none effect. The counsel of the Lord standeth forever, the thoughts of his heart to all generations."† Again,—"There are many devices in a man's heart; nevertheless the counsel of the Lord, that shall stand."‡ From these and a multitude of similar passages, it is clear that God has many purposes concerning this world, and concerning men; and that all those purposes will certainly be fulfilled. Indeed the most important prophecies of the Old and New Testaments are not so much predictions of what *will come to pass,* as revelations of what God *has purposed to bring to pass.*

But what was the *great purpose* for which our world was created? The Scriptures teach us, that the great end of creation was the manifestation of the glory of God. "The Lord," says Solomon, "hath made all things for himself."§ And holy beings around the throne of God, sing,—"Thou art worthy, O Lord, to receive glory, and honor and power; for thou hast created all things, and for thy pleasure they are and were created."‖

But though all the works of God declare his glory, it

---

* Isai. 46: 9, 10. † Ps. 33: 10, 11. ‡ Prov. 19: 21.
§ Prov. 16: 4 ‖ Rev. 4· 11.

was by *man*, created in his moral image, that God designed chiefly to manifest his glory. "The *final cause* of man's creation," as the Rev. Richard Watson, a Methodist writer, well remarks, "was the display of the glory of God, and principally his moral perfections."* But how is God to be glorified by man? Before they were created, God foresaw the fall of the human race into sin. He could not have designed, therefore, that they should glorify him by continuing in a state of holiness. Accordingly we are taught in the Scriptures, that Christ "was foreordained before the foundation of the world" to become the Saviour of fallen men. And Paul the Apostle uses the following language on this subject: "Unto me, who am less than the least of all saints, is this grace given, that I should preach among the Gentiles the unsearchable riches of Christ; and to make all men see what is the fellowship of the mystery, which from the beginning of the world hath been hid in God, who created all things by Christ Jesus: to the intent that now unto the principalities and powers in heavenly places might be known by the church the manifold wisdom of God, according to the eternal purpose which he purposed in Christ Jesus our Lord."†

From this language we learn, that God from eternity purposed to manifest to his rational creatures his manifold wisdom by means of the church redeemed by Jesus Christ, and that in fulfillment of this purpose he created all things by Him. Even Watson, though a decided Arminian, says,—"The redemption of man by Christ was certainly not an after-thought brought in upon

---

* Theol. Inst, pt. 2, ch. 18.

† Eph. 3: 8-11,

man's apostasy; it was a *provision*, and when man fell, he found justice hand in hand with mercy."* We are warranted, then, in the conclusion, that God from eternity designed this world to be the theatre on which he would display his manifold wisdom by the redemption of fallen men.

For the accomplishment of this glorious design God has governed the world from the beginning, and will govern it to the end. When our Saviour gave his Apostles the great commission to go and teach all nations, he said,—"All power is given unto me in heaven and in earth." And Paul teaches us, that Christ is now "far above all principality, and power, and might, and dominion, and every name that is named, not only in this world, but also in that which is to come;" and that God "hath put all things under his feet, and given him to be head over all things to the church." And for the salvation of his church, "he must reign, until he hath put all enemies under his feet." We can never understand the providence of God over our world, unless we regard it as a complicated machinery, having ten thousand parts, directed in all its operations to one glorious end,—*the display of the manifold wisdom of God in the salvation of the Church of Christ.* And even when viewed in this Scriptural light, there are many things too deep for our limited powers; and we are obliged to exclaim, as did Paul concerning the dispersion of the Jews,—"O the depth of the riches both of the wisdom and knowledge of God! how unsearchable are his judgments and his ways past finding out!"

---

* Theol inst. pt. 2, ch. 18.

The *government* of the world is naturally divided into the government of *matter* and the government of *mind*. Concerning the former, there is no dispute among Christians. While all agree that God governs matter, in some sense, by fixed laws, all must admit that he so interposes as to send his blessings or his judgments upon his creatures as his infinite wisdom dictates. At one time he sends the early and the latter rain, and blesses the land with fruitful seasons; at another, he curses it with drought and famine. Now he commissions the breezes to bear upon their bosoms the blessings of health; then he loads them with pestilential vapors, spreading death and mourning in their course. How he exerts this controlling influence over matter, we know not; but that he does so, no one who believes the Scriptures, can doubt.

But the most important, as well as the most difficult part of this subject, relates to the government of *mind*. To what extent and by what influence does God govern men and angels? They are divided into two classes,—the righteous and the wicked; and they perform two classes of actions,—the good and the bad.

I. Perhaps most professing Christians will admit, that God is, in an important sense, the author of all pure affections and actions. The holy angels he created in his own image, as he created man; and he has preserved them in holiness. Since the fall, all men are born into the world *totally depraved*. In this truth the more evangelical class of Arminians agree with us; and as we design not now to argue with those who deny the fundamental doctrines of Christianity, we shall not stop to prove the doctrine of *original sin*, but shall take it as admitted. Now it is evident, that from a totally depraved heart pure affections and actions cannot proceed.—Consequently whatever of holiness there is in any human being, must proceed from the Spirit of God. And so teaches the inspired Paul. He enumerates the Christian virtues, as love, joy, peace, long-suffering, gentleness, goodness, faith, meekness, temperance, and pronounces them all "the fruit of the Spirit."* And all the good works of men he teaches us to regard as effects of regeneration. "For we are his workmanship created in Christ Jesus unto good works, which God hath before ordained, that we should walk in them."† And when he exhorts Christians to work out their salvation, he adds;—"for it is God which worketh in you both to will and to do of his good pleasure."‡

Beside that influence by which the heart is sanctified, God exerts upon good men a *directing* influence, by which they are guided through life. "The steps of a good man are ordered by the Lord: and he delighteth in his way."§ What Solomon says of men generally, is especially true of those over whom the good Shepherd exercises a particular care,—"Man's goings are of the Lord: how can a man then understand his own way?"‖ *How* God exerts upon the human mind a sanctifying and controlling influence without interfering with its free agency and accountability, we cannot explain; but that he does so, is too clear to be disputed.

But what shall we say of the government which God exercises over *wicked men* and their actions? To answer

---

* Gal. 5: 22, 23. † Eph. 2: 10. ‡ Phil. 2: 12. 13,
§ Ps 37: 23. ‖ Prov. 20: 24.

this question satisfactorily we must inquire into the origin of sin in our world. Our first parents were created in the moral image of God, and were placed on probation in the garden of Eden, "having the law of God written in their hearts, and power to fulfil it; and yet under a possibility of transgressing, being left to the liberty of their own will, which was subject unto change." They were tempted by Satan; they yielded to the temptation, and fell; and all their posterity were involved in the fall. Consequently all men are now born in total depravity, being entirely destitute of holiness and disposed only to sin.

Now let it be understood, we deny that God exerted, or purposed to exert any influence on the minds of our first parents, *inclining them to sin.* Our Confession teaches distinctly, that they were "left to the liberty of their own will," and were endowed with power to fulfil the requirements of God.* Calvin taught, that man in his primitive state possessed reason, understanding, prudence and judgment, not only for the government of his life on earth, but to enable him to ascend even to God and eternal felicity; that to these was added choice to direct the appetites, and regulate all the organic motions, so that he was entirely conformed to the government of reason; that in his integrity he was endued with free will, by which, if he had chosen, he might have obtained eternal life; and that Adam could have stood if he would, since he fell merely by his own will.†

In what sense, then, did God foreordain the fall of man? The Westminster Confession answers this ques-

*Westminster Confession, ch. 4. † Inst., Book 1, ch. 15.

tion in the following language: "Our first parents, being seduced by the subtilty and temptation of Satan, sinned in eating the forbidden fruit. This their sin God was pleased, according to his wise and holy counsel, to permit, having purposed to order it to his own glory."* God, who knew all things, knew that Satan would tempt our first parents, and that the temptation would be successful. This he knew perfectly, when he created them, and placed them in the garden of Eden; and, as the Rev. Richard Watson admits, he had, even before the fall, made provision for the redemption of the human race. It will not be pretended, that God could not have prevented Satan from entering the garden, and tempting Eve; nor will any one say, that he was indifferent to the fate of the first pair and all of their posterity. We cannot avoid the conclusion, therefore, that for wise reasons God was pleased to endow man with just such powers as he gave him and no greater, to place him in the circumstances in which Satan found him, and to permit Satan successfully to tempt him. That God permitted the temptation knowing it would be successful, is certain; and that he had wise reasons for such permission, is equally clear. And inasmuch as all things were created for his glory, we hold (and who will venture to deny it?), that he purposed to order this sin to his glory, in connection with the plan of redemption. Our doctrine, then, concerning the first sin committed by man, and in which the human race was involved, is simply, that God for wise reasons decreed or purposed,

* Ch. 6.

first, to *permit*, and, secondly, to *overrule* it for his glory.

As Adam stood in his trial as the representative of his posterity, the whole race fell in his fall ; and the consequences of his sin passed upon them as well as upon him. Richard Watson teaches, that the *death* threatened as the penalty of Adam's transgression included "corporeal, moral or spiritual, and eternal death ;" that "the sentence included also the whole of his posterity;" and consequently all are born in a state of spiritual death or of total depravity.* We do not believe, however, that *original sin*, in which all are born, consists in any depravation of the soul, or the infusion of any positive evil. The confessions of the Reformed Churches all of which are decidedly Calvinistic, teach, as the Rev. Dr. Hodge states, "that original righteousness, as a punishment of Adam's sin, was lost, *and by that defect* the tendency to sin, or corrupt disposition, or corruption of nature, is occasioned." And the same able writer agrees with President Edwards, "that the absence of positive good principles, and the withholding of special divine influence, and the leaving of the common principles of self-love, natural appetite, which were in man in innocence, are sufficient to account for all the corruption which appears among men."†

We have now clearly before us the Calvinistic view of the origin of sin, so far as the human race is concerned, and of the total depravity in which all are born. God created the world, and placed man in it for his own

---

* Theol. Inst., pt. 2, ch. 18. † Com. on 5th ch. of Rom.

glory. He purposed to display his manifold wisdom by means of the Church redeemed by the blood of Christ. He, therefore, purposed to *permit* the temptation and the fall of our first parents, and to leave their posterity, deprived of original righteousness, to the workings of their own minds and hearts. All, therefore, are dead in sin.

We are now prepared to inquire into the nature of the government or control which God exercises over wicked men. This is a most important question; for God governs wicked men for the purpose of accomplishing his holy ends; and the influence he now exerts upon them, is precisely the influence which from eternity he purposed to exert. The influence which he exerts upon wicked men, is of *four* kinds, viz:

1. A *restraining* influence, by which they are prevented from doing what they are naturally inclined to do. Thus God said to Abimelech, king of Gerar, who took Sarah from Abraham,—"For I also withheld thee from sinning against me: therefore suffered I thee not to touch her."* And to encourage the Jews to attend their three annual festivals at Jerusalem, he said,—"Neither shall any man desire thy land, when thou shalt go up to appear before the Lord thy God thrice in the year."† He promised, during their attendance on their festivals, to restrain the covetous desires of their pagan neighbors.

2. God often exerts on the minds of wicked men what we may call a *softening* influence, disposing them, contrary to their natural inclination, to do that which will promote his cause. Cyrus, king of Persia, was a pagan and a wicked man; yet in order that the prophecy in

---

* Gen. 20: 6. † Exod. 34: 24.

Jeremiah might be fulfilled, "the Lord stirred up the spirit of Cyrus, king of Persia, that he made a proclamation throughout all his kingdom," in favor of the rebuilding of the temple in Jerusalem.* And when Artaxerxes afforded the Jews aid in the same work, Ezra said,—"Blessed be the Lord God of our fathers, which hath put such a thing as this in the king's heart, to beautify the house of the Lord which is in Jerusalem: and hath extended mercy unto me before the king, and his counsellors, and before all the king's mighty princes."†

3. God exerts on the minds of wicked men a *directing* influence, so that good is made to result from their intended evil. The brethren of Joseph hated him, and determined to kill him. This wicked design God prevented through the instrumentality of Reuben, whose heart was softened. In the absence of Reuben, certain Ishmaelitish merchants passed by; and God permitted them to sell Joseph to them. They were wicked men, and were, therefore, willing to enslave a noble youth for the sake of gain; but God in his providence so ordered things, that they were on their way to Egypt,—the country to which he purposed to send Joseph,—and that they passed by just at the right time. That the hand of God was in this event and in those which, in the same connection, preceded and followed it, we know; for Joseph said to his brethren,—"God sent me before you, to preserve you a posterity in the earth, and to save your lives by a great deliverance."‡ This *directing* influence, which God exerts over wicked men, is constantly spoken of in the Scriptures. Of the proud king of Assyria, God

* Ezra 1: 1. † Ezra 7: 27, 28. ‡ Gen. 45: 7.

said,—"I will send him against a hypocritical nation, and against the people of my wrath will I give him a charge, etc. Howbeit he meaneth not so neither doth his heart think so."* Solomon says,—"A man's heart deviseth his way: but the Lord directeth his steps."† And again,—"The king's heart is in the hand of the Lord, as the rivers of water: he turneth it whithersoever he will."‡ Jeremiah says,—"O Lord, I know that the way of man is not in himself: it is not in man that walketh to direct his steps."§

4. There is a sense in which God *hardens* the hearts of wicked men, and blinds their minds. When God commanded Moses to perform miracles in the presence of Pharaoh, and to require him, in the name of the God of Israel, to let his people go, he said,—"But I will harden his heart, that he shall not let the people go."‖ And when Pharaoh and his army pursued the Jews to the Red Sea, God bade them go forward, and said,—"Behold, I will harden the hearts of the Egyptians, and they shall follow them; and I will get me honor upon Pharaoh, and upon all his host, upon his chariots, and upon his horsemen."¶ When the Spirit of the Lord departed from Saul, king of Israel, "an evil spirit from the Lord troubled him."** When God would send Ahab to battle to be slain, Micaiah the prophet said, "The Lord hath put a lying spirit in the mouth of all these thy prophets, and the Lord hath spoken evil concerning thee."†† Concerning the rebellious Jews who rejected the Saviour, it is said,—"He hath blinded their eyes, and hardened their heart; that they should

* Isai. 10: 6, 7. † Prov. 16: 9. ‡ Prov. 21: 1. § Jer. 10: 23.
‖ Exod. 4: 21. ¶ Exod. 14: 17. ** 1 Sam. 16: 14. †† 1 Kings 22: 23.

not see with their eyes, nor understand with their heart, and be converted, and I should heal them."*

But these and similar declarations of the Scriptures, we do not understand, as already stated, that God exerts an influence upon the hearts of men, *disposing* them to feel and act wickedly. Pharaoh's heart was hardened, as we believe, first, by his being given up of God to his evil dispositions, as were the heathen of whom Paul speaks;† and, secondly, by the repeated and, to him, irritating command to give up without compensation the enslaved people of God. Saul was given up of God, and left to be tempted and tormented by the devil. Ahab, unwilling to believe the true prophets, was abandoned to be deluded and ruined by false prophets. The unbelieving Jews were left to themselves, and were consequently both hardened and blinded. But in all these cases, God had wise purposes to accomplish, and as the Psalmist had said, the wrath of man was made to praise him; and the remainder of wrath he restrained.‡

II. The doctrine of Divine decrees, then, may be briefly summed up as follows: 1. God, from eternity, purposed to govern matter as he is now governing it, in accordance generally with fixed laws. 2. God is properly the author of all true holiness in men, and he produces such holiness according to his eternal purpose. 3. God chose to *permit* some angels and all the human race to fall into sin, and so to overrule their dispositions, softening, restraining, directing, hardening, as to bring good out of evil, to accomplish his all-wise purposes.

And this is the doctrine, as taught in the Westminster

---

* John 12: 40. † Rom. 1. ‡ Psalm 76: 10.

Confession of Faith. "God from all eternity did by the most wise and holy counsel of his own will, freely and unchangeably foreordain whatsoever comes to pass; yet so as thereby neither is God the author of sin; ncr is violence offered to the will of the creatures, nor is the liberty or contingency of second causes taken away, but rather established."* But how is this? If God has foreordained whatsoever comes to pass, how is it that he is not the author of sin? The answer to this question may be found in the chapters on the fall of man and on providence. Of the fall of man, the Confession, as we have already seen, says;—"This their sin God was pleased, according to his wise and holy counsel, to permit, having purposed to order it to his own glory." Two things only did God purpose to do concerning the fall of man, viz: to *permit* it, and to *overrule* it for good. In the chapter on providence we read,—"The almighty power, unsearchable wisdom, and infinite goodness of God, so far manifest themselves in his providence that it extendeth itself to the first fall, and all other sins of angels and men, and that not by a bare permission, but such as hath joined with it a most wise and powerful bounding, and otherwise ordering and governing of them, in a manifold dispensation, to his own holy ends; yet so as the sinfulness thereof proceedeth only from the creature, and not from God; who being most holy and righteous, neither is, nor can be, the author or approver of sin." God fulfils his decrees by his *providential* and *gracious* influences. With the sinful actions of angels and men, his *providential* influence only is con-

* Westmin. Conf., ch. 3

cerned. He *permits* their sinful dispositions, but does not *produce* them. Yet he does more than barely to permit; he bounds, directs, restrains and controls their actions to his own holy ends. And inasmuch as he simply permits and controls the sinful actions of men, he is not the author or approver of sin. There is nothing inconsistent in the idea, that God hated the treachery of Judas and the cruelty of the Jews toward our Saviour, and that he yet so overruled their conduct, that his name was glorified, and the salvation of an innumerable multitude secured. It is certain, that they did only what his hand and his counsel determined before to be done.* "And indeed," as Calvin well remarks, "unless the crucifixion of Christ was according to the will of God, what becomes of our redemption?" The doctrine of Divine decrees, as held by the Presbyterian Church and by all enlightened Calvinists, is stated by the late venerable Dr. Green, in his lectures on the Shorter Catechism, in the following language: "All events, of whatever kind, that take place in time, were determined, or foreordained by God from all eternity, thus to take place; and all for the ultimate promotion of his own glory. It ought, however, to be carefully noted here, that all who soundly hold this doctrine, maintain that there is a difference always to be kept up between what have been denominated the *efficacious decrees* and the *permissive decrees* of God. His efficacious decrees relate to whatever is *morally good;* his permissive decrees to whatever is *morally evil.* In other words, his *immediate agency*, according to his decree, is concerned

* Acts 4: 27, 28.

in whatever is morally good,—his immediate agency is *never* concerned in what is morally evil. Evil he permits to take place, and efficaciously overrules it for good,—for the promotion of his glory."* The doctrine is very clearly expressed in the following language of Augustine, quoted with approbation by Calvin: "That they sin, proceeds from themselves; that in sinning they perform this or that particular action, is from the power of God, who divideth the darkness according to his pleasure."† That is, God *permits* men to have sinful dispositions and affections; but for his own glory he so *directs* their course, that he brings good out of their intended evil. The doctrine is perfectly expressed by Solomon, when he says;—"A man's heart deviseth his way; but the Lord directeth his steps."‡

The Westminster Confession teaches further, that "Although God knows whatsoever may or can come to pass, upon all supposed conditions; yet hath he not decreed anything because he foresaw it as future, or as that which would come to pass, upon such conditions." God foresaw, that our first parents would yield to the temptation presented by Satan; but he did not purpose to permit the temptation and the fall, because he foresaw it as that which would come to pass. He might have foreseen, that if the temptation were presented, Eve would yield; and he might have purposed to prevent the temptation. But for wise reasons he chose to permit both the temptation and the fall, designing to overrule both to his own holy ends. God did not purpose to send Joseph into Egypt, because he foresaw that his brethren would hate

* Vol. 1, pp. 180, 181. † Institutes, b. 2, ch, 4. ‡ Prov. 16: 9.

him and sell him, and that the Ishmaelitish merchants would readily buy him. He might have foreseen, that such results would follow under the circumstances; and he might have purposed to deliver Joseph out of their hands. But he had a great and benevolent purpose to accomplish; and, therefore, he so ordered events, that the Ishmaelitish merchants were passing by just when Joseph had been thrown into a pit by his vindictive brethren. God did not decree the crucifixion of his Son, because he foresaw that wicked men would crucify him; but he decreed it because it was necessary to the salvation of men. God has revealed his purpose, on the day of judgment, to pronounce sentence of condemnation upon the wicked "for their sin." He did not form the purpose to condemn them, because he foresaw that he would condemn them; but because he foresaw that they would live and die in sin, and because the ends of justice would require their condemnation.

This explanation of the doctrine will, we are confident, remove the difficulties by which, when incorrectly viewed, it has seemed to many to be pressed. The correct statement of it, it will be perceived, destroys the whole force of the objections most plausibly urged against it.

CHAPTER III.

THE DOCTRINE OF DIVINE FOREORDINATION PROVED BY THE WORD OF GOD.

HAVING carefully stated the doctrine of Divine decrees, as held by Presbyterians and by Calvinists generally, we now proceed to inquire more particularly, whether it is taught in the Word of God. For the sake of getting a clear view of the doctrine, it has been properly divided into two parts, viz: The general purposes of God, and the particular purposes relating to the salvation of men; or, in brief, *Decrees* and *Election*. The most of what we shall say in this chapter, will be on the former branch of the subject; though the providence and the efficacious grace of God do often so meet and mingle, that it may not be possible to keep them entirely distinct.

That, in the sense already explained, God did from all eternity foreordain whatsoever comes to pass, is clearly proved by the following considerations:

I. *The providence of God extends to all events, or to whatsoever comes to pass.* The infinitely wise Jehovah has created nothing that is worthless, and no creature of his is beneath his regard. Of all his creatures it is said,—"These wait all upon thee, that thou mayest give them their meat in due season. That thou givest them, they gather: thou openest thy hand, they are filled with good. Thou hidest thy face, they are troubled, thou takest away their breath, they die, and return to their dust."* Our Saviour encouraged his disciples to rely for temporal blessings upon the providence of God, by assuring them, that it extends to the fowls of the air, and even to the lilies of the field. "Behold the fowls of the air: for they sow not, neither do they reap, nor gather into barns; yet your heavenly Father feedeth them. Are ye not much better than they?"† By a similar consideration he encouraged his Apostles to trust confidently in the divine protection, while engaged in their difficult and perilous mission. "Are not two sparrows sold for a farthing? and one of them shall not fall on the ground without your Father. But the very hairs of your head are all numbered. Fear ye not, therefore, ye are of more value than many sparrows."‡ Every blessing we enjoy, we are taught to regard as a gift of God,§ and every affliction we suffer, as a judgment, or a parental chastisement designed for our good.‖ In the Lord's prayer we are taught to ask for daily bread, thus acknowledging a superintending providence over all the means by which, and the sources from which, it is obtained; and we are taught to pray for deliverance from temptation and evil, thus acknowledging the Divine control of all things and persons whose influence can tempt, and whose power can injure us. Accordingly pious men have ever been accustomed gratefully to acknowledge the goodness of God in their blessings, and humbly to bear their trials as parental chastisements. If Abraham's pious servant had occa-

* Ps. 104: 27–29. † Matt. 6: 26. ‡ Matt. 10: 29–31.
§ James 1: 17. ‖ Heb. 12: 5–11.

sion to speak of the greatness and the wealth of his master, he said,—"The Lord hath blessed my master greatly; and he is become great: and he hath given him flocks and herds, and silver and gold,"* etc. If Jacob became wealthy in spite of the dishonesty of his father-in-law, he said,—"God hath taken away the cattle of your father, and given them to me."†

The same providential control over the minds and actions of men, which is implied in some of the passages already quoted, is directly taught in many others. When Nehemiah desired permission to leave Babylon, and go and build Jerusalem, being cup-bearer to the king, he must obtain his permission. He, therefore, prayed,—"O Lord, I beseech thee, let now thine ear be attentive to the prayer of thy servant and to the prayer of thy servants who desire to fear thy name; and prosper, I pray thee, thy servant this day, and grant him mercy in the sight of this man."‡ And when Artaxerxes rendered the Jews important assistance in rebuilding and beautifying the temple, Ezra thus gave thanks: "Blessed be the Lord God of our fathers, which hath put such a thing as this into the king's heart, to beautify the house of the Lord which is in Jerusalem: and hath extended mercy unto me before the king, and his counselors, and before all the king's mighty princes."§ Joseph, while a prisoner in Egypt, became a favorite of the keeper; and the inspired historian says,—"The Lord was with Joseph, and showed him mercy, and gave him favor in the sight of the keeper of the prison."‖

* Gen. 24: 35. † Gen. 31: 9. ‡ Neh. 1: 11.
§ Ezra 7: 27, 28. ‖ Gen. 39: 21.

The Scriptures teach us, that the *wicked actions* of men, no less than the *virtuous*, are wholly under the Divine control. If Pharaoh, king of Egypt, stubbornly refused to obey the command to let the Israelites go, the Lord hardened his heart.* When the anger of the Lord was kindled against Israel "he moved David against them to say, Go, number Israel and Judah;" and the desolating pestilence followed.† Because of the sin of Solomon, God purposed to separate ten of the tribes of Israel from his kingdom, and give them to Jeroboam, one of his servants. Ahijah the prophet, said to Jeroboam,—"For thus saith the Lord, the God of Israel, Behold, I will rend the kingdom out of the hand of Solomon, and will give ten tribes to thee." When Rehoboam his son succeeded to the throne, the people demanded a milder government, and promised allegiance to him, if their request were granted. The integrity of the kingdom now depended upon this decision. He took three days to consider the matter. He consulted the old counselors, who had stood before his father, and they advised him to grant the request of the people. He took counsel with the young men who were his associates, and, following their advice, he answered the people harshly, refusing their request, and threatening to increase their burdens. The result was, the revolt of the ten tribes. The inspired writer explains this remarkable event in the following language: "So the king hearkened not unto the people: for the cause was of God, that the Lord might perform his word, which he spake by the hand of

* Exod. 7.

† 2 Sam. 24: 1.

Ahijah the Shilonite to Jeroboam the son of Nebat."* We need no better illustration, and no stronger confirmation, than is here afforded, of the language of the Westminster Confession, viz: "God from all eternity did by the most wise and holy counsel of his own will, freely and unchangeably ordain whatsoever comes to pass; yet so as thereby neither is God the author of sin; nor is violence offered to the will of the creatures, nor is the liberty or contingency of second causes taken away, but rather established." That God had ordained the revolt of the ten tribes, and the reign of Jeroboam over them, is absolutely certain; for he had revealed the purpose before the event occurred. Yet Rehoboam was left free to consider all the motives which might influence his conduct; and his advisers, old and young, were free in the counsel they respectively gave. All the contingencies naturally attending such events, attended this. And yet such was the final decision, that the purpose of God was fulfilled; and the inspired writer could say with truth, "the cause was of God, that he might perform his word." When God would destroy Ahab the wicked king of Israel in battle, Micaiah the prophet said,—"Now, therefore, behold, the Lord hath put a lying spirit in the mouth of these thy prophets, and the Lord hath spoken evil against thee."†

These historical facts, to which others will be added in the course of this discussion, do strikingly illustrate and confirm the general truth taught in such passages of Scripture as the following: "A man's heart deviseth his way: but the Lord directeth his steps." "The

* Comp. 1 Kings 11: 29–32, and 2 Chron. 10. † 2 Chron. 18: 22.

king's heart is in the hands of the Lord, as the rivers of water: he turneth it whithersoever he will." "There are many devices in a man's heart: nevertheless the counsel of the Lord, that shall stand."* "O Lord, I know that the way of man is not in himself: it is not in man that walketh to direct his steps."† "Surely the wrath of man shall praise thee: the remainder of wrath shalt thou restrain."‡ All these passages teach with perfect clearness the free agency and accountability of man, and the sovereignty of God in bringing to pass his wise purposes. Men form their plans, and form them freely; but God bounds, overrules and directs.

The providence of God, then, extends to the wants and lives of all his creatures, even the most worthless of them; to the lives and wants especially of his rational creatures; and still more especially of his children; and to the actions, good and bad, of all men. Is it not clear, therefore, that the providence of God extends to all things?—that "He worketh all things after the counsel of his own will?"§

It is the doctrine of a particular providence, that gives to the righteous a feeling of security in the midst of danger; that gives them assurance that the path of duty is the path of safety and of prosperity; and that encourages them to the practice of virtue, even when it exposes them to the greatest reproach and persecution. How often, when clouds and darkness seem to gather over them, do they rejoice in the assurance given by their Saviour, "I will never leave thee, nor forsake

* Prov. 6: 9; 21: 1; 19: 21.
† Jer. 10: 23.
‡ Ps. '6: 10.
§ Eph. 1: 11.

thee." How often have they, when overwhelmed with troubles and afflictions, taken fresh courage as they have read the language of Paul,—"We know that all things work together for good to them that love God, to them who are the called according to his purpose." Where is the Christian who would willingly give up this precious doctrine?

On this subject I am happy to find myself sustained by some of the most eminent Arminians. JOHN WESLEY has a sermon on *Divine Providence,* preached from the text, "Even the very hairs of your head are all numbered." He says,—"The doctrine of Divine providence has been received by wise men in all ages;" and it is impossible to use stronger language than he does in asserting a *particular* providence. After asserting and proving, that God created all things, sustains all things, sees and knows all the properties of the beings He has made, he writes as follows:

"And is the creator and preserver of the world unconcerned in what he sees therein? Does he look upon these things either with a malignant or heedless eye? Is he an Epicurean god? Does he sit at ease in the heavens, without regarding the poor inhabitants of earth? It cannot be. He hath made us; not we ourselves; and he cannot despise the work of his own hands. We are his children: and can a mother forget the children of her womb? Yea, she may forget; yet will not God forget us! On the contrary, he hath expressly declared, that as his 'eyes are over all the earth,' so he 'is loving to every man: and his mercy is over all his works.' Consequently he is concerned every moment, for what befalls every creature upon earth; and more especially for everything that befalls any of the children of men. It is hard, indeed, to comprehend this: nay, it is hard to believe it; considering the complicated wickedness, and the complicated misery, which we see on every side. But believe it we must, unless we will make God a liar; although it is sure, no man can comprehend it. It behooves us, then, to humble ourselves before God, and to acknowledge our ignorance. Indeed, how can we expect that a man should be able to comprehend the ways of God! Can a worm comprehend a worm? How much less can it be supposed, that a man can comprehend God:

'For how can finite measure infinite?'"

Mr. Wesley very forcibly and conclusively exposes the doctrine of a general, but not particular providence. "You say," says he, "you allow a *general* providence, but deny a *particular*. And what is a general, of whatever kind it be, that includes not particulars? Is not every general necessarily made up of its several particulars? Can you instance in any general that is not? Tell me any genus, if you can, that contains no species? What is it that constitutes a genus, but so many species added together? What, I pray, is a whole that contains no parts? Mere nonsense and contradiction. Every whole must, in the nature of things, be made up of its several parts; insomuch that if there be no parts, there can be no whole." Again:—"Do you mean (for we would fain find out your meaning, if you have any meaning at all), that the providence of God does, indeed, extend to all parts of the earth, with regard to great and singular events; such as the rise and fall of empires; but that the little concerns of this or that man are beneath the notice of the Almighty? Then you do not consider, that *great* and *little* are merely relative terms, which have place only with respect to men. With regard to the Most High, men, and all the concerns of men, are nothing, less than nothing, before him. And nothing is small in his sight, that, in any degree, affects the welfare of any that fear God and work righteousness. What becomes, then, of your general providence, exclusive of a particular? Let it be forever rejected by all rational men, as absurd, self-contradictory nonsense. We may then sum up the whole Scriptural doctrine of providence, in the fine saying of St. Austin,—'*Ita præsidet singulis sicut universis, et universis sicut singulis.*'"*

I am truly gratified to find in the writings of Wesley a statement so clear, and a defense so conclusive and unanswerable, of the doctrine, *that the providence of God extends to all things and to all events.*

II. *God in his providence is simply fulfilling his purposes.* This truth is so obvious, and the denial of it so absurd, that it is scarcely necessary to say a word in confirmation of it. The acts of providence, by which individuals are controlled and particular events brought to pass, are either *accidental* or *designed.* But no one, it is presumed, could for a moment entertain the belief of an *accidental* providence. All, therefore, must admit that whatever God does in the government of the world, he does *designedly.* For example, Joseph said to his brethren, "God did send me before you to preserve life."† Now Joseph was sent to Egypt, not by *miracle,*

* He rules over particulars as over universals, and over universals as over particulars.

† Gen. 45: 5.

5

but by the overruling *providence* of God. If, then, God in his providence sent him into Egypt, he did it in fulfillment of a previously-formed purpose; and therefore it is stated, that the sending of Joseph to Egypt was a *means* to accomplish a wise and benevolent *end*, viz: to preserve life. But a wise being first determines upon the end he desires to attain, and then upon the best means of accomplishing it. God determined to preserve the lives of Jacob's family; and he purposed to send Joseph before them to Egypt for the accomplishment of this object. God in his providence sent the Jews into captivity at Babylon; but he did so for their good, that in exile they might consider their ways and repent. In his providence he restored them at the end of seventy years; and he made Cyrus to fulfill his gracious purpose.

But surely I need not argue this point. An accidental providence, is an absurdity; and if it could exist, it would neither be good nor wise; nor could it afford to the righteous any ground of confidence. The Scriptures, therefore, distinctly teach that God "worketh all things *according to the counsel of his will*;" that although the heart of a man deviseth his way, "the Lord directeth his steps;" that "his tender mercies are over all his works." In this view Mr. Wesley agrees with Calvinists, as we have already seen. He spurns the idea that God looks upon his creatures with indifference, and maintains most earnestly that he wisely and mercifully rules over and cares for them, even the smallest of them.

Now let us pause and determine to what conclusion we are constrained to come, from the preceding argument. The providence of God extends to all things and to all events,—to whatsoever cometh to pass; and God is, in his providence, simply fulfilling his purposes. In both these positions Mr. Wesley agrees with us; but from them the conclusion inevitably follows, *that God hath foreordained whatsoever cometh to pass*. Look at the premises. If the providence of God extends to whatsoever comes to pass; and if his providence is nothing more nor less than the fulfilling of his purposes; is it not perfectly clear, that his purposes extend to whatever comes to pass? For illustration, you say of an architect, his work extends to every part of the building; and in his work he is simply carrying out his plans or purposes. Does it not follow that his plans extend to every part of the building? And is it not then true, that he did previously plan what he executed? One of three positions we are compelled to take on this subject. 1. We may deny a particular providence; and then, as Wesley demonstrates, we deny a providence altogether. 2. We may hold to an *accidental* providence,—if such a thing be conceivable,—that God in the government of the world acts without design, and consequently without wisdom or goodness. 3. We may hold that he governs all things according to his wise counsels, for the accomplishment of his own glorious ends; or, in other words, that he hath foreordained whatsoever cometh to pass. Look carefully at the positions, and see whether you are not obliged to take one of the three; and if so, choose between them. Which is Scriptural? Which is most honorable to God? Which is safest and most encouraging to the righteous? I verily believe, that no Christian will long hesitate which of the propositions he must choose.

III. *The purposes of God are* ETERNAL. To this proposition, if the two preceding are admitted, there can be no objection. For if it be in perfect consistency with the wisdom and goodness of God, that his purposes should extend to all things and events ; why should not those purposes have been formed before the creation of the world ? Who ever charged it as crime against a man, that he had *too soon* determined to do a good work ? If it was wise and merciful in our Heavenly Father to send Joseph into Egypt, who can say it is inconsistent with his perfections that he always designed to do this wise and good act? And if the fact that God has foreordained whatsoever comes to pass, either destroys man's free agency or makes him the author of sin (and these questions will be fully examined in another chapter), these results follow as certainly if the decrees are formed *one hour* or *one moment* before they are executed, as if they were formed before the beginning of time. If the free agency of Cyrus was destroyed by God's foreordaining that he should take Babylon and restore the Jews, it matters not whether that decree was formed at the moment when Isaiah recorded it, or ten thousand ages before.

But that all the purposes of God are eternal, is clear from the following considerations :

1. *He is infinitely wise,* knowing all things,—past, present and future; all things *possible* as well as all things *real.* The declarations of the Scriptures on this subject are as strong as language can make them.

"Known unto God are all his works from the beginning of the world;" or, as the Rev. Richard Watson, a standard Methodist writer, happily gives the sense of the passage,—"Rather *ap' aionos,* from all eternity,—known, before they were made, in their *possible,* and known, now they are made, in their *actual* existence."* "Great is the Lord, and of great power: his understanding is infinite."† Arminians have no difficulty in admitting that God knows, with infinite accuracy, all things and events that are past or present, and all those yet future, not dependent upon, or immediately connected with, the *free actions of accountable beings.* But they have been accustomed to assert, that the doctrine of Divine decrees is destructive of the free agency and accountability of man; and many of them have felt an equal difficulty in reconciling the Divine foreknowledge with free agency. I am happy to be able, on this point, to call in the aid of the distinguished Methodist writer just now quoted,—especially as his Theological Institutes are considered by the Methodists a standard work. Some Arminians have held, that "it is a matter of choice in God to think of finite ideas." "In substance," says Mr. Watson, "these opinions are, that though the knowledge of God be infinite, as his power is infinite, there is no more reason to conclude that his knowledge should be always exerted to the full extent of its capacity, than that his power should be employed to the extent of his omnipotence; and that if we suppose him to *choose* not to know some contingencies, the infiniteness of his knowledge is not thereby impugned." To this Mr.

* Theol. Inst., pt. 2, ch. 4.

† Ps. 147: 5.

Watson gives the following conclusive answer: "1. That the infinite power of God is in Scripture represented, as in the nature of things it must be, as an infinite *capacity*, and not as infinite in act; but that the *knowledge* of God is, on the contrary, never represented there to us as a capacity to acquire knowledge, but as *actually* comprehending all things that are, and all things that can be. 2. That the notion of God's choosing to know some things, and not to know others, supposes a *reason* why he refuses to know any class of things or events, which reason, it would seem, can only arise out of their nature and circumstances and therefore supposes at least a partial knowledge of them, from which the reason for his not choosing to know them arises. The doctrine is therefore somewhat contradictory."

A second theory, stated by Watson, is "that the foreknowledge of contingent events, being in its own nature impossible, because it implies a contradiction, it does no dishonor to the Divine Being to affirm that of such events he has and can have no prescience whatever; and thus the prescience of God as to moral actions being wholly denied, the difficulty of reconciling it with human freedom and accountability has no existence." To this and the foregoing theory Mr. Watson gives the following unanswerable refutation: "To this the same answer must be given as to the former. It does not meet the case, so long as the Scriptures are allowed to contain prophecies of rewardable and punishable actions. That man is accountable to God for his conduct, and therefore free, that is, laid under no invincible necessity of acting in a given manner, are doctrines clearly contained in the Bible; and the notion of necessity has here its full and satisfactory reply; but if a difficulty should be felt in reconciling the freedom of an action with the prescience of it, it affords not the slightest relief to deny the foreknowledge of God as to actions in general, while the Scriptures contain predictions of the conduct of men whose actions cannot have been determined by invincible necessity, because they were actions for which they received from God a just and marked punishment. Whether the scheme of relief be that the knowledge of God, like his power, is arbitrary, or that the prescience of contingencies is impossible, so long as the Scriptures are allowed to contain predictions of the conduct of men, good or bad, the difficulty remains in all its force. The whole body of prophesy is founded on the prescience of contingent actions, or it is not prediction, but guess and conjecture,—to such fearful results does the denial of the Divine prescience lead."*

It is, then, clear from the Scriptures, and Mr. Watson admits and proves it, that God knows all the past, the present, and the future. The conclusion to which we must come, in view of this doctrine, is that the purposes of God are eternal. For intelligent purposes are not formed at random, but are founded upon knowledge. Therefore every new purpose formed by a rational being, and every change of purpose, must be founded on new knowledge gained. A man determines to-day to go on a journey to a distant city, or to enter upon an extensive speculation. Why is this purpose formed to-day and not before? Because he has gained information to-day which he had not yesterday. Or, having last week

* Theol. Inst., pt. 2, ch. 4.

determined to go to Boston, he this week changes his purpose. Why? Because he has views now, which he had not when the purpose was formed. Every new purpose formed, therefore, and every change of purpose, proclaims the imperfection of him who forms or changes the purpose. His knowledge was imperfect; he has learned something new, and, therefore, has formed a new purpose, or abandoned one previously formed. But God learns nothing new. All the reasons in view of which his purposes were formed, were before the Divine Mind, and were perfectly understood from eternity. There can be nothing, consequently, on which a new purpose can be founded; and to maintain that he forms new purposes, is to maintain that he is an imperfect Being,—that he does not know all things.

2. *When the inspired writers speak of the formation of the Divine purposes, they speak of them as* ETERNAL. Is Jesus Christ sent into the world to save men? He "verily was foreordained before the foundation of the world."* Does God bless his children with all spiritual blessings? He does so "according as he hath chosen us in him, before the foundation of the world."† He does so "according to his own purpose and grace, which was given us in Christ Jesus before the world began."‡ Will he display his manifold wisdom by his Church? He will do it "according to the eternal purpose which he purposed in Christ."§

Now let us put these three propositions together, and see to what conclusion we are obliged to come. The providence of God extends to all things and all events.

* 1 Pet. 1: 20. † Eph. 1: 4.
‡ 2 Tim. 1: 9. § Eph. 3: 11.

God in his providence is simply fulfilling his purposes. Therefore his purposes extend to all things and all events. His purposes are eternal. Therefore he from eternity purposed to do what in time he is doing. That is, he from eternity foreordained whatsoever comes to pass.

> "Ten thousand ages ere the skies
> Were into motion brought;
> All the long years and worlds to come,
> Stood present to his thought,
> There's not a sparrow nor a worm,
> But's found in his decrees,
> He raises monarchs to their thrones,
> And sinks them as he please."

CHAPTER IV.

Objections to the doctrine of divine foreordination answered, and the inconsistencies of Arminianism pointed out.

The evidence appears conclusive, that, according to the Scriptures, God hath foreordained whatsoever cometh to pass. Against this doctrine, however, several objections are urged. Let us give them a careful consideration.

1. This doctrine, it is confidently affirmed, is inconsistent with *the free agency and accountability of man.* Those who press this objection, must, if they are consistent, hold the doctrine of man's free ageney,—must believe that such is the nature of the human mind, that it is capable of choosing and refusing. Free Agency is nothing more nor less than *acting without compulsion, and in accordance with one's desires or inclinations.* The mind is free, if it is capable of considering the motives to action which may be placed before it, and of choosing its own course. The word *motives* is sometimes used to signify the *reasons* or *inducements* placed before the mind, tending to lead to certain choices or actions; and sometimes, to designate the *feelings* under which men make certain choices, or perform certain actions. Used in the former sense, that which would be a powerful motive in the view of one mind, would be no motive at all in the view of another. The offer of a bribe would be a sufficient

motive to induce one judge to decide a case contrary to law and evidence ; while to another, such an offer, so far from being a motive to such a course, would be highly offensive. The temptation presented by Potiphar's wife, which was firmly resisted by Joseph, would have been a motive of sufficient power to have ruined many a youth of less purity of heart. An *external* motive can have no influence over the choices and conduct of men, except as it makes an appeal to feelings existing in the mind ; and all the affections of the human heart are, in their very nature, *free*. The idea of *compelling* a man either to love or to hate any object, is perfectly absurd. We hold, then, that man is, from the very nature of his mind, a free moral agent,—that he is capable of looking at all the motives presented before him, and of acting, in view of them all, freely and without compulsion. That every one will choose what, on the whole, he prefers, is certain. To assert the opposite, would be a contradiction in terms. It would be the same as to say, that the mind chooses what, on the whole, it does not prefer, or does not choose. But all the choices of the intelligent mind are free and unconstrained.

Now if man's free agency is destroyed in any case, it must be by some *force ab extra,—from without,* which is brought to bear upon the mind. This will not be disputed. Suppose, then, the doctrine true, that God has foreordained whatever comes to pass, does this foreordination bring such a *force* to operate on the mind ?

The government of the world, as we remarked in a preceding chapter, is naturally divided into the government of *matter* and of *mind.* Among men there are two classes,—the righteous and the wicked. As we have proved, God is, in an important sense, the author of all the *pure affections* and *virtuous actions* of men. The righteous are declared to be "his workmanship, created in Christ Jesus unto good works."* And "it is God which worketh in you both to will and to do of his good pleasure."† And concerning all that is truly good in any man, he must say, with the Apostle Paul,—"But by the grace of God I am what I am."‡ Now, that God can and does exert on the minds of men a supernatural purifying influence, producing virtuous affections and prompting to virtuous actions, the more evangelical class of Arminians admit and teach. In the Articles of Religion adopted by the Methodist Episcopal Church, we find the following language: "The condition of man after the fall of Adam is such, that he cannot turn and prepare himself, by his own natural strength and works, to faith, and calling upon God; wherefore we have no power to do good works, pleasant and acceptable to God, without the grace of God by Christ preventing us, that we may have a good will, and working with us when we have that good will." This influence of Divine grace, as our Methodist brethren believe, results in multitudes of instances in the conversion of men from the service of sin and Satan to the service of God; and they of course hold, that the free agency of the persons is not thereby destroyed or impaired. They therefore agree with us, that God can and does exert upon the minds of men a supernatural influence, which in a great number of instances results in their regeneration, and that their free agency is left unimpaired. Now, the only

---

* Eph. 2: 10. † Phil. 2: 13. ‡ 1 Cor. 15: 10.

question necessary to be decided here is, whether without interfering with the free agency of man God can exert such an influence as will *certainly* lead to conversion in all cases where it is put forth; for if he can, he can fulfill all his purposes concerning the salvation of men without interfering with their freedom. Mr. A., for example, under the preaching of the gospel, was convicted of sin, and, in a few days, became a converted man and a happy Christian. Our Methodist brethren will agree with us in ascribing his conviction and his regeneration to the supernatural influence of the Holy Spirit. The influence which God graciously exerted on his mind, was sufficient, and God knew it would be sufficient, to lead him to Christ. But here is Mr. B. Can God, without interfering with his free agency, exert upon his mind an influence which will lead to the same result? Who will venture to say, he cannot? Perhaps it will be said, a more powerful influence will be necessary to bring Mr. B. to repentance, than was required in the case of Mr. A. Let us for the present admit that it may be so. Then the matter presents itself to us thus:—that Divine influence which is necessary to bring the mind of Mr. A. to a certain state, is perfectly consistent with his free agency; but that Divine influence, somewhat greater, which is necessary to bring the mind of Mr. B. to the same state, is destructive of his free agency. Now, upon what principle of philosophy or of Scripture can any one make such an assertion? Is it not evident, that if the greater influence on the mind of Mr. B. would destroy his freedom of choice, the lesser influence on the mind of Mr. A. would produce the same effect,—the only difference being, that the freedom of the latter is more easily destroyed than that of the former?

But all that is said about the destruction of man's free agency by Divine influence, is mere *assertion* without a particle of evidence. No man knows *how* the Spirit operates on the human heart; and therefore no man can possibly know how far such operation is consistent with freedom of choice. "The wind bloweth where it listeth, and thou hearest the sound thereof, but canst not tell whence it cometh, and whither it goeth; so is every one that is born of the Spirit."* The Scriptures nowhere authorize the assertion, that God cannot quicken whom he will; and all assertions of the kind are both unfounded and irreverent. Admitting, as our Methodist friends do, a supernatural influence terminating in many cases in the regeneration of men, it certainly devolves on them to prove that God cannot, without impairing their freedom, exert an influence which will so result in all cases. We might, then, with propriety ask them to tell us precisely what amount or degree of supernatural influence is consistent with free agency. Can any one fix the limit? If not, how can he determine when that limit is passed?

So far, then, as the virtuous affections and actions of men are concerned, the doctrine of Divine Decrees is not liable to the charge of destroying the free agency of man. Indeed the language of the Scriptures is calculated to rebuke all such attempts to limit the power of Divine grace. "We are his workmanship;" says

* John 3: 8.

Paul, "created in Christ Jesus unto good works." Regeneration is here represented as a *new creation.* Does the thing created assist in its own creation? Or does it require a greater power to perform one creative act than another? The same apostle says,—"Even when we were dead in sins, God hath quickened us together with Christ." Does the being who is quickened or made alive, assist in his own quickening? Did Lazarus co-operate in raising himself from the dead? Or does it require greater power to impart life to one being than to another? But as the discussion of this subject comes more properly under the head of *Election,* the fuller consideration of it will be reserved for the second part of this work.

But it is asserted that the doctrine under consideration destroys the free agency of *sinners,* and makes God the author of their sins. And in enforcing this objection, the following questions are pressed, viz: Can anything possibly come to pass which God has not foreordained?—and, Can anything which he has foreordained fail to come to pass? These questions we of course answer in the negative; and then we are asked, How can men be free in their choices and actions, when they could do nothing more and nothing less than they in fact do? Men often confuse their own minds, as well as the minds of others, by using, with reference to the exercises of the mind, language which is borrowed from material bodies. If it is said, that nothing *can* happen which was not foreordained, the idea of *compulsory* influence is immediately attached to the words *can* and *cannot.* But our Arminian brethren, at least many of them, believe that God does with infinite certainty foreknow all the events that will ever come to pass, the free actions of men as well as all others. Now let us ask them the same question they press upon our attention, viz : Can anything possibly come to pass which God has not foreknown ? — and, Can anything fail to come to pass which he has foreknown ? They must answer these questions in the negative ; and then we may ask them, How then can the choices and actions of men be free, when they do only what was infallibly foreknown, and what, therefore, they could not but do ?

But all such reasoning is fallacious. As we have already remarked, if the free agency of men is destroyed, it must be by some *external force* brought to act upon their minds, which are naturally free. The question then arises,—Does the doctrine of Divine foreordination imply any such force upon the minds of wicked men ? Or in other words,—Can God exert upon the minds of wicked men such an influence as to bring to pass by their instrumentality his own wise and holy purposes without interfering with their free agency and just accountability ? If any one assert that he cannot, we ask him to prove the truth of his assertion, either from reason or from the Bible.

As we have already stated, God, in order to fulfill his purposes, exerts upon the minds of sinful men a *restraining* influence, a *softening* influence, a *directing* influence, and a *hardening* influence. Now let us inquire, whether by either of these influences the free agency of men is destroyed or impaired.

God often *restrains* men from doing that to which their natural appetites or passions strongly incline them.

Thrice in the year all the males of the Jews were required to attend the annual festivals in Jerusalem. To encourage them to do this, God said,—"For I will cast out the nations before thee, and enlarge thy borders: neither shall any man desire thy land, when thou shalt go up to appear before the Lord thy God thrice in the year."* On this passage, Matthew Henry, has the following note: "All hearts are in God's hands, and under his check; he can lay a restraint not only upon men's actions, but upon their desires. Canaan was a desirable land, and the neighboring nations were greedy enough; and yet God says 'they shall not desire it.'" Abimelech, king of Gerar, sent and took Sarah, Abraham's wife, while they sojourned with him. And when he protested that he was not aware of doing what was unlawful, God said, "Yea, I know that thou didst this in the integrity of thy heart; for I also withheld thee from sinning against me: therefore suffered I thee not to touch her."† On this passage, Henry thus appropriately remarks: "It is God that restrains men from doing the ill they would do; it is not from him that there is sin, but it is from him that there is not *more* sin, either by his influence upon men's minds, checking their inclination to sin, or by his providence, taking away the opportunity to sin." God purposed that Abraham and his wife should dwell safely in Gerar; and therefore, while he permitted the king to send to take Sarah to his palace, he restrained him from proceeding further. Now in what manner God exerted this restraining influence, we cannot comprehend; and

* Exod. 34: 24. † Gen. 20: 6.

therefore, it is impossible for us to have any evidence that it interfered with Abimelech's freedom of choice. But since the Scriptures clearly teach that such an influence was exerted, the objection that it interferes with free agency lies against the Scriptures themselves, not simply against Calvinism; aud therefore, it is an objection which cannot be consistently urged by those who believe in the inspiration of the Bible.

2. God often exerts on men what may be called a *softening* influence, disposing them to do what is according to his will and for the glory of his name. Thus he gave Joseph favor with the keeper of the prison where he was confined. Thus, that he might fulfill his decree concerning the restoration of the Jews and the rebuilding of the temple, he "stirred up the spirit of Cyrus, king of Persia," that he made a proclamation throughout all his kingdom, in which he used the following remarkable language: "The Lord God of heaven hath given me all the kingdoms of the earth; and he hath charged me to build him a house at Jerusalem, which is in Judah. Who is there among you of all his people? his God be with him, and let him go up to Jerusalem, which is in Judah, and build the house of the Lord God of Israel (he is the God), which is in Jerusalem."* And at a later period, God put it into the heart of Artaxerxes to beautify the temple, and to favor the labors of Ezra.† It mattters not, so far as the doctrine of Divine Decrees is concerned, what *instrumentalities* were employed in affecting the hearts of these sinful men. The fact is clear, that God had certain important purposes to accom-

---

* Ezra 1: 1–3. † Ezra 7: 27, 28.

plish, and that he brought such influences to bear upon their minds, as lead them to aid in the fulfillment of his purposes. *How* these influences were exerted, no one can comprehend; and, therefore, no one can have the least evidence that they impaired the free agency of the men upon whom they were exerted. And if any one persist in asserting the incompatibility of such influences with human accountability, his controversy is with the Bible, not with Calvinism.

3. God exerts upon men a *directing* influence. The same affection or passion in the human mind might lead to the performance of any one of fifty acts, or to any one of several courses of conduct. A man, for example, is *ambitious*. There are many ways in which he may have the prospect of gratifying his ambition,—as by the accumulation of wealth, by filling important civil offices, by military exploits, by literary attainments, etc. Now the peculiar character of his ambition, and the circumstances in which he may by placed, will determine his course of action; and if God in his providence arrange these circumstances, he will thereby direct his course of conduct. A man is *covetous;* but there are many ways in which his love of money may be gratified. He may labor industriously; he may speculate boldly; he may gamble; he may become a highway robber. "The love of money," says Paul, "is the root of all evil." It is the prolific source from which crimes of all kinds proceed. Now, what course of conduct a covetous man will pursue, depends upon the influences under which his moral character is formed, and the circumstances that surround him. We hold not that God produces avaricious feelings

in the heart of such a man, but that he gives such direction to his conduct that good and not evil shall result. The Ishmaelitish merchants who purchased Joseph and sold him to Potiphar, were avaricious men; but God gave such direction to their conduct, that by their instrumentality he sent Joseph into Egypt, and thus made them instruments in fulfilling a most important purpose.

Now, will any one venture the assertion that God cannot exert a directing influence over the conduct of wicked men without destroying or impairing their free agency? Without understanding the nature of that influence, no one can assert or deny in the matter; and no one can understand it. If, however, any one persist in the objection, his quarrel is with the Word of God which teaches abundantly that such influence is exerted. Of this we have given some evidence, and will furnish more before closing this chapter.

4. God is said sometimes to *harden* the hearts of men, and thus to accomplish his purposes. Concerning Pharaoh, king of Egypt, God said: "Even for this same purpose have I raised thee up, that I might show my power in thee, and that my name might be declared throughout all the earth."* In carrying out this purpose God said: "I will harden his heart, that he shall not let the people go."† Pharaoh was a wicked man, but was doubtless, like other wicked men, restrained and softened in some degree by divine influence. God chose now to withdraw that influence and leave him to himself, while yet he commanded him to let his people go; and thus he hardened his heart. But was Pharaoh's

* Exod. 9: 16. † Exod. 4: 21.

free agency destroyed by his being left to his own will? To say so, would be ridiculous; for if the human mind is naturally free, it of course never enjoys liberty more complete than when left to itself. And equally ridiculous would it be to assert that because he was left to his own will, and God overruled his wicked designs for good, he was not free.

It is, then, perfectly clear, I think, that neither of these four classes of Divine influences interferes in the slightest degree with man's free agency and accountability; and by these are all the decrees of God connected with the agency of wicked men fulfilled. We have abundant evidence in God's word, that he can and does so control wicked men as to bring to pass his purposes. "The king's heart is in the hand of the Lord, as the rivers of water: he turneth it whithersoever he will."* Now, it will not be pretended either that kings are not free and accountable beings, or that He who can turn the king's heart whithersoever, he will, cannot as easily turn the hearts of others. "A man's heart deviseth his way: but the Lord directeth his steps."† If the Lord can direct the steps of men, and yet leave their hearts free to devise their way, it is clear that he can so control their conduct that his purposes will be accomplished without infringing their liberty. We have in the tenth chapter of Isaiah's prophecy, a remarkable proof and illustration of the doctrines of Divine Decrees and Free Agency. "O Assyrian, the rod of mine anger, and the staff in their hand is mine indignation. I will send him against a hypocritical nation, and against the people of my

* Prov. 21: 1. † Prov. 16: 9.

wrath will I give him a charge, to take the spoil, and to take the prey, and to tread them down like the mire of the streets. Howbeit he meaneth not so, neither doth his heart think so; but it is in his heart to destroy and cut off nations not a few. For he saith, Are not my princes altogether kings? etc. Wherefore it shall come to pass, that when the Lord hath performed his whole work upon Mount Zion and on Jerusalem, I will punish the fruit of the stout heart of the king of Assyria, and the glory of his high looks. For he saith, By the strength of my hand I have done it, and by my wisdom; for I am prudent, etc. Shall the ax boast itself against him that heweth therewith? or shall the saw magnify itself against him that shaketh it? as if the rod should shake itself against them that lift it up, or as if the staff should lift up itself, as if it were no wood." What is the obvious meaning of this language? It does most unequivocally teach, in the first place, that the king of Assyria, though a proud and ungodly man, was an instrument in the hands of God, just as the ax, the saw, or the rod in the hands of a man, to execute his purposes upon the Jews; and that God had perfect control of him. It teaches, in the second place, that the free agency of the king was not destroyed or impaired by this control, but that he was perfectly free to form his own plans and to be governed by his own desires. For it is declared that he did not design to execute God's purposes, but to promote his own ambitious projects. "Howbeit he meaneth not so, neither doth his heart think so; but it is in his heart to destroy and cut off nations not a few." It consequently teaches, thirdly, that the king was justly held accountable for his pride and wickedness, although God so overruled him that he fulfilled his wise purposes. God decreed to chastise the Jews for their sin. He chose to employ the king of Assyria to execute his purpose, and therefore *sent* him against them. He would afterward punish the king for his wicked plans. Is it not evident, then, beyond all cavil, that the Scriptures teach that God can and does so control men, even wicked men, as to bring to pass his wise purposes without interfering with their free agency? The objection we are considering is, therefore, wholly without force.

Again: The Scriptures contain many examples both confirmatory and illustrative of the truth that God can and does fulfill his purposes by the instrumentality of even wicked men, and consequently of the consistency of Divine Decrees and Free Agency. One of the most remarkable of these examples is found in the history of Jacob's family, already referred to. Let us look, first, at the decree, and then at its fulfillment. God said to Abram,—"Know of a surety that thy seed shall be a stranger in a land that is not theirs, and shall serve them; and they shall afflict them four hundred years. And also that nation whom they shall serve, will I judge: and afterward shall they come out with great substance."* Here is the *decree.* The descendants of Abraham were to go and sojourn, and be afflicted in Egypt. How was this decree fulfilled? There are a number of links in the chain of its fulfillment. The first is the partiality manifested by Jacob for Joseph, the son

* Gen. 15: 13, 14.

of his old age. The second link is the consequent hatred of Joseph's brethren. The third is his dreams, which increased their hatred. The fourth is his being sent by his father to see how they were doing, and his following them to the place to which they had removed their flocks. When they saw him coming, they conspired to murder him, but were prevented by Reuben. He was placed in a pit; and just then came along Ishmaelitish merchants going to Egypt. Joseph is sold to them, and by them to Potiphar, an officer of Pharaoh. He is slandered and thrown into prison, where, the Lord giving him favor with the keeper, he meets with Pharaoh's two servants, and interprets their dreams; and thus ultimately he becomes known to Pharaoh, and becomes the second man in authority in Egypt.

Now Joseph said, that *God sent him* to Egypt to preserve many lives.* He sent him in fulfillment of a benevolent purpose. *How* did he send him? By the instrumentality of a number of persons, good and bad. God permitted his brethren to hate him. He so ordered things, that the merchants passed along just at the proper time, and were going to the country to which he purposed to send Joseph; and he permitted them to sell him. Link after link of the chain of events is formed, and everything is overruled to the entire fulfillment of God's purpose. And yet it will not be pretended, that Joseph's brethren, and the others who were actors in this chain of events, were deprived of their freedom, nor that their guilt was at all diminished by the fact that God brought great good out of their intended evil.

* Gen. 45: 7.

Joseph said to them,—"But as for you, ye thought evil against me; but God meant it unto good, to bring to pass, as it is this day, to save much people alive."* In the exercise of their free agency they formed their purposes, and they were evil; but God also had his purposes, and they were good. They deserved condemnation, and they condemned themselves for their sin; but God was to be praised for his merciful designs. Throughout this interesting history, we have the most striking illustrations of the perfect harmony of divine sovereignty and free agency. It is truly astonishing that any one who has ever read it with attention, should urge the objection we are now considering.

Mr. Watson says, "It was predicted that Babylon should be taken by Cyrus in the midst of a midnight revel, in which the gates should be left unguarded and open;" and he argues, that "all the actions which arose out of the warlike disposition and ambition of Cyrus," were foreknown, "because the result of them was predicted."† Now it is rather singular, that it did not occur to Mr. Watson, that the taking of Babylon by Cyrus was not predicted simply as an event which God *foresaw*, but as an event which he had *foreordained.* Of the destruction of Babylon, Isaiah employs the following language: "The burden of Babylon, which Isaiah the son of Amoz did see. Lift ye up a banner upon the high mountain, exalt the voice unto them, shake the hand, that they may go into the gates of the nobles. I have commanded my sanctified ones, I have also called my mighty ones for mine anger, even them that rejoice

* Gen. 50: 20.

† Theol. Inst., pt. 2, ch. 4.

in my highness. The noise of a multitude in the mountains, like as of a great people; a tumultuous noise of the kingdoms of nations gathered together: the Lord of hosts mustereth the host of the battle. They come from a far country, from the end of heaven, even the Lord, and the weapons of his indignation, to destroy the whole land."* Again:—"For I will rise up against them, saith the Lord of hosts, and cut off from Babylon the name, and remnant, and son, and nephew, saith the Lord. I will also make it a possession for the bittern, and pools of water: and I will sweep it with the besom of destruction, saith the Lord of hosts. The Lord of hosts hath sworn, saying, Surely as I have thought, so shall it come to pass; and as *I have purposed,* so shall it stand: That I will break the Assyrian in my land, and upon my mountains tread him under foot: then shall his yoke depart from off them, and his burden depart from off their shoulders. This is *the purpose that is purposed* upon the whole earth: and this is the hand that is stretched out upon all nations. For the Lord of hosts *hath purposed,* and who shall disannul it? and his hand is stretched out, and who shall turn it back?"† Jeremiah, describing the same terrible event, says:—"For every *purpose* of the Lord shall be performed against Babylon, to make the land of Babylon a desolation without an inhabitant."‡ Not only the destruction of Babylon, but the instruments by which, and the manner in which, it should be accomplished, were foreordained. "Behold," saith God, "I will stir up the Medes against them, which shall not regard silver."

* Isai. 13: 1–5. † Isai. 14: 22–27. ‡ Jer. 51: 29.

"Go up, O Elam: besiege, O Media," etc.* Of Cyrus, God said :—"He is my shepherd, and shall perform all my pleasure: even saying to Jerusalem, Thou shalt be built; and to the temple, Thy foundation shall be laid." But before Cyrus could restore the Jews, and cause the city of Jerusalem and the temple to be rebuilt, he must conquer Babylon, and take possession of it. And therefore God said :—"Thus saith the Lord to his anointed, to Cyrus, whose right hand I have holden, to subdue nations before him; and I will loose the loins of kings, to open before him the two-leaved gates, and the gates shall not be shut; I will go before thee, and make crooked places straight: I will break in pieces the gates of brass, and cut in sunder the bars of iron: And I will give thee the treasures of darkness, and hidden riches of secret places, that thou mayest know that I, the Lord, which call thee by thy name, am the God of Israel. Foı Jacob my servant's sake, and Israel mine elect, I have even called thee by thy name: I have surnamed thee, though thou hast not known me."† From these and other explicit declarations of prophecy, it is evident beyond all controversy, that the taking of Babylon by an army of Medes and Persians, commanded by Cyrus, and the return of the Jews to Jerusalem by permission and decree of Cyrus, were foreordained; and so, of course, were all the counsels and acts which led to these results. It is certain that these events were foreordained; and consequently we are obliged to conclude, either that the doctrines of Divine Decrees and Free Agency are perfectly consistent, or that all the persons

---

* Isai. 13: 17; 21: 2. † Isai. 44: 28; 45: 1–4.

by whose instrumentality these events were brought to pass, were deprived of their free agency and accountability. Indeed, Mr. Watson himself, forgetting surely what he had elsewhere written, admits that "Cyrus was *elected* to rebuild the temple."* In making such an admission, he has unwittingly overthrown the most plausible argument urged by Arminians against the doctrine of Divine foreordination. For if God's election of Cyrus to fulfil his purposes relative to the Jews did not interfere with the free agency of Cyrus, the election of any other man or number of men to fulfil any other of the Divine purposes would leave them as free as Cyrus. Our Arminian opponents must either deny that God ever foreordained any one event brought about by a free agent, or abandon the objection we are considering.

The Lord Jesus Christ was crucified by wicked men; and yet no one, it would seem, can doubt that his crucifixion was foreordained. Upon that event hung the hopes of a lost world. Every bleeding victim on the Jewish altar foretold the sufferings of the great Antitype, and all the prophets predicted the great event. Peter declares that he "verily was foreordained before the foundation of the world" to this work;† and to the Jews he said:—"Him, being delivered by the determinate counsel and foreknowledge of God, ye have taken, and by wicked hands have crucified and slain."‡ And the apostles, in their prayer for protection against their persecutors, use this remarkable language: "For of a truth against thy holy child Jesus, whom thou hast

---

* Theol. Inst., pt. 2, ch. 26. † 1 Pet. 1: 20. ‡ Acts 2: 23.

anointed, both Herod, and Pontius Pilate, with the Gentiles, and the people of Israel, were gathered together, for to do whatsoever thy hand and thy counsel determined before to be done."* Precisely in accordance with these declarations, is the language of Isaiah:— "Yet it pleased the Lord to bruise him; he hath put him to grief."† It is absolutely certain that the crucifixion of Christ was foreordained, and that in his crucifixion the Jews and Romans did but fulfil the Divine purpose; and yet it is certain that they were in the perfect exercise of their free agency. The crucifixion of Christ was, therefore, charged upon them as a crime; and they were commanded to repent of it. They meant evil against him; but God intended good. He made the wrath of man to praise him; and the remainder of wrath he restrained.

I might multiply, to any extent, examples of events certainly foreordained, yet brought to pass by the free and accountable agency of men; but it is unnecessary. One example is as good as ten thousand; for if, in one single instance, men have fulfilled the decree of God, and were yet free and accountable, it is certain that the decrees of God are not inconsistent with man's free agency. The objection we are considering, is consequently without the least force. Let it be distinctly understood, that they who urge this objection must deny that *any one event* brought to pass by the free agency of man, was foreordained! Is any Christian prepared for this? Mr. Watson asserts, that the whole body of prophecy is founded upon the prescience of the free or

* Acts 4: 27, 28. † Isai. 53: 10.

contingent acts of men. With more truth he might have said, that the whole body of prophecy was founded on the *foreordination* of the free acts of men; for prophesy is, for the most part, but the revelation of God's purposes concerning individuals and nations.

Here we might let the argument rest; but the objection under consideration has been so often and so plausibly urged, that we are determined to sift it to the bottom and expose its weakness.

If God has foreordained whatsoever comes to pass, it is maintained, man is not a free agent, but acts from necessity. As we have more than once remarked, if the freedom of the human mind is destroyed or impaired, it must be by some *force from without;* because it is naturally free. Now what is there in a *purpose* or *decree* of God, which brings such a force to bear? Let us, if you please, analyze a Divine decree, and see if we can find in it such a force. In a decree of God we may find three things, viz: the *decree* or *purpose itself,* as it exists in the Divine Mind; the *certainty of the event* decreed; and *the manner* in which, or the influence by which, it is brought to pass.

Let us first consider the decree or purpose *itself.* A Divine Decree, as already, explained, so far as rational creatures are concerned, is a determination by God to dispose them to do something good, or to permit and overrule their evil acts to his own holy ends. Such a purpose, we will say, God has formed. It exists in the Divine Mind; but it has not been revealed, nor has any single act in accordance with it been put forth. Now is it not self-evident, that so long as that purpose remains in the Divine Mind, not revealed nor acted upon, it cannot bring a *force* to bear upon the mind of any man? If God had even determined to influence or dispose Pharaoh to hate and oppress the Israelites, still that purpose could not have affected his free agency, until some *act* was put forth. The purpose itself effects nothing, just as the purpose of a man to build a house effects nothing until some act is put forth in accordance with the purpose. This is too plain to require illustration, or to admit of proof.

But it may be said, if God has decreed an event, it will certainly come to pass; and if it is certain and cannot be otherwise, how can man be free to act or not to act in reference to it? To this objection we have two answers to make: 1. There is no *force* in mere certainty; and therefore the simple fact that an event will certainly happen, cannot put a force upon the mind which will destroy or impair its liberty. 2. If the certainty of a future event is inconsistent with the free agency of those employed in bringing it to pass, then the *foreknowledge of God* destroys that free agency; for whatever actions or events are foreknown, will certainly come to pass. The Saviour foreknew that Judas would betray him; for "as they did eat, he said, Verily I say unto you, that one of you shall betray me."* And he foreknew that Peter would deny him; for he said to him, "Verily, I say unto thee, that this night, before the cock crow, thou shalt deny me thrice."† Both of these events were absolutely certain. The former, indeed, was foretold a thousand years before Judas was born.‡ Was the free agency of Judas and Peter destroyed? They certainly

* Matt. 26: 21. † Matt. 26: 34. ‡ Acts 1: 16.

did not think so, for Judas said: "I have sinned in that I have betrayed the innocent blood."* "And Peter remembered the word of Jesus, which said unto him, Before the cock crow, thou shalt deny me thrice. And he went out, and wept bitterly."† The crucifixion of Christ was foreknown and foretold; and Paul says:—"They that dwell at Jerusalem, and their rulers, because they knew him not, nor yet the voices of the prophets which are read every Sabbath-day, they have fulfilled them in condemning him. And when they had fulfilled all that was written of him, they took him down from the tree, and laid him in a sepulchre."‡ Did the certainty of his crucifixion destroy or impair the freedom of those who fulfilled, though they knew it not, all that was written of him? It is clear as the shining light, that the certainty of a future event interferes not with the free agency of those by whose instrumentality it will be brought to pass.

Here again we are happy to call to our aid the Rev. Richard Watson, who, as we have seen, contends earnestly and conclusively for the doctrine, that God does certainly foreknow all the free actions of his creatures, and unanswerably refutes the absurd and mischievous theories of Dr. Adam Clarke and others, who deny such prescience. "The whole body of prophecy," he remarks, "is founded on the certain prescience of contingent actions, or it is not prediction, but guess and conjecture,—to such fearful results does the denial of the Divine prescience lead! No one can deny that the Bible contains predictions of the rise and fall of several king-

* Matt. 27: 4. † Matt. 26: 75. ‡ Acts 13: 27, 29.

doms; that Daniel, for instance, prophesied of the rise, the various fortune, and the fall of the celebrated monarchies of antiquity. But empires do not rise and fall wholly by immediate acts of God; they are not thrown up like new islands in the ocean, they do not fall like cities in an earthquake, by the direct exertion of Divine power. They are carried through their various stages of advance and decline, by the virtues and vices of men, which God makes the instruments of their prosperity or destruction. Counsels, wars, science, revolutions, all crowd in their agency; and the predictions are of the combined and ultimate results of all these circumstances, which, as arising out of the vices and virtues of men, out of innumerable acts of choice, are *contingent.* Seen they must have been through all their stages, and seen in their results, for prophecy has registered those results. The prescience of them cannot be denied, for that is on record; and if certain prescience involves necessity, then are the daily virtues and vices of men not contingent. It was predicted that Babylon should be taken by Cyrus in the midst of a midnight revel, in which the gates should be left unguarded and open. Now, if all the actions which arose out of the warlike disposition and ambition of Cyrus were contingent, what becomes of the principle that it is impossible to foreknow contingencies? * * * Our Lord predicts most circumstantially, the destruction of Jerusalem by the Romans. If this be allowed, then the contingencies involved in the conduct of the Jews who provoked that fatal war, — in the Roman Senate who decreed it,—in the Roman Generals who carried it on,— in the Roman and Jewish soldiers who were engaged in it,—were all *foreseen*, and the result of them *predicted*: if they were not contingencies, that is, if they were not free actions, then the virtues and vices of both parties, and all the acts of skill, and courage, and enterprise, and all the cruelties and sufferings of the besieged and the besiegers, arising out of innumerable volitions, and giving rise to the events so circumstantially marked in the prophesy, were determined by an irreversible necessity." Mr. Watson concludes, that "though an *uncertain* action cannot be foreseen as certain, a free, unnecessitated action may; for there is nothing in the knowledge of the action, in the least, to affect its nature."* The *certainty* of a future event, then, as Mr. Watson agrees with Calvinists, cannot interfere with the freedom of those by whose agency it is brought to pass.

The only other thing in a Divine decree is *the manner* in which, or *the agency* by which the event decreed is brought to pass. And if the doctrine of Divine Decrees is destructive of free agency, this is the point where the difficulty occurs. Here, if anywhere, a compulsory force is brought to bear upon the mind. Indeed it is only the certainty that the necessary *means* will in due time, be employed, that makes any foreordained event certain. All the purposes of God concerning men are fulfilled either by his *providence* or by his *regenerating and sanctifying grace*. Christ Jesus is "head over all things to the Church;" and the Holy Spirit is sent to convince and convert men, that they may enter the Church. All God's purposes, therefore,

* Theol. Inst., pt. 2, ch. 4.

are fulfilled by that particular providence which, as we have seen, extends to all things and to all events, or by that blessed Spirit who works in his people to will and do.

The whole matter, therefore, resolves itself into the two questions: 1. *Can God exercise over men a particular providence, so as to bring to pass his wise purposes, without destroying or impairing their free agency?* 2. *Can God exert upon the minds of men, providentially and by his Spirit, a Divine influence that will certainly lead them o Christ, and induce them to persevere in his service, without interfering with their liberty?* These questions have already been answered. We have seen, that the providence of God extends to all things and events, and that he can so govern even wicked men as to fulfill his purposes without interfering with their freedom of choice. We have seen, too, that he does exert on the minds of men a supernatural sanctifying influence, "working in them to will and to do of his good pleasure," yet leaving their free agency unimpaired. It is clear, therefore, that the decrees of God do not interfere with the free agency of men.

It has been too generally admitted, I cannot but think, by Calvinists, that we cannot reconcile the doctrines of Divine Decrees and Free Agency. It has been common to insist, that since both these doctrines are taught in the Scriptures, they are certainly true, and therefore consistent, and ought to be received, though we, with our limited powers and knowledge, cannot see how they harmonize. This position is certainly tenable; for there evidently are many things presented in nature and in revelation, which, as to the *mode* of their being, and as to their consistency with other things equally clear, are above human comprehension. But it is not wise to admit even an *apparent* inconsistency in the doctrines under consideration, unless truth and candor require it.

Now I cheerfully admit, that there is in this general subject something to us incomprehensible ; but I insist, and am prepared to prove, that the difficulty lies, not against the points on which Arminians differ from us, but against those in reference to which they agree with us. That a mere purpose existing in the Divine mind, not yet revealed or acted out, cannot interfere with the free agency of any one, is self-evident; for it brings no force of any kind to bear upon the mind. It is equally clear, that the mere certainty of a future event does not impair the freedom of those by whose agency it will be brought to pass. The certainty that Cyrus would take Babylon, did not interfere with his free agency in planning and executing his wars. The certainty that Peter would deny the Lord, did not interfere with his liberty and accountability in that act. On this point, as we have seen, the Rev. Richard Watson precisely agrees with us. If, then, the free agency of men is destroyed, this is done not by the divine purposes abstractly considered, nor by the certainty of the events decreed, *but by the influences by which those purposes are fulfilled.* But all the purposes of God concerning men, are fulfilled either by his particular providence or by the renewing and sanctifying influence of the Holy Spirit. The question, therefore, concerning the consistency of Divine Decrees and Free Agency, as already remarked, resolves itself into the two following questions, viz: 1. Can God exercise over men a particular providence without interfering with their freedom? 2. Can he renew and sanctify the hearts of men without impairing their liberty? The first of these questions the Rev. John Wesley, the father of Methodism, answers in the affirmative, as we have already shown, strongly insisting upon the doctrine of a particular providence over all men and things. And the Rev. Richard Watson contends for the renewing influence of the Holy Spirit. Precisely at this point the difficulty occurs. Let any one explain to me, how a particular providence and a divine influence on the hearts of men are consistent with free agency, and I pledge myself to explain how the doctrine of divine purposes is consistent with free agency. How did God so order things that Cyrus took Babylon and restored the Jews, without interfering with the liberty of those who fulfilled his purposes? How did he send Joseph into Egypt without impairing the liberty of those by whose instrumentality the result was brought about? How does God quicken those dead in trespasses and sins, and work in his people to will and to do, without interfering with their liberty? Answer these questions, and I will at once show how Divine Decrees and Free Agency are reconcilable. The difficulty is not concerning *the divine purposes*, but concerning *a particular providence and divine influence* on the hearts of men. But Arminians, at least many of them, hold both these doctrines. The difficulty, therefore, arises not about points on which they differ from us, but concerning Divine providence and Divine influence, in reference to the existence of which they agree with us.

Let it, then, be distinctly understood, that our Arminian friends must either withdraw the objection, that the doctrine of Divine Decrees is destructive of free agency, or they must deny the doctrines of a particular providence and divine influence. For it is by a controlling providence, and divine influence that all the purposes of God concerning the conduct of men, are fulfilled; and if the free agency of men is destroyed, it is by these influences. We must, then, charge the Arminian system with being wholly inconsistent with the fundamental doctrines of Divine providence and Divine influence. God in his providence fulfills his purposes; and if his purposes destroy free agency, he cannot exercise a providence over men; much less can he "work in them to will and to do of his good pleasure."

Now think what would be the condition of our world, if there were no providence and no divine influence upon the hearts of men. Deny these doctrines, and what is left that is better than blank Atheism? But our Arminian friends will not reject them; they earnestly contend for them. If, then, they will not be chargeable with gross inconsistency, they must withdraw the objection, that Divine Decrees are destructive of Free Agency. The doctrines which they hold, labor under the precise difficulty they charge upon ours.

The plain truth on this whole subject is, that we know absolutely nothing concerning the manner in which God operates on the human heart; and therefore we can know nothing at all concerning the consistency of the divine operations with human freedom, save what we learn from the Scriptures and from our own consciousness. From neither of these sources do we learn, that God cannot so control men as to fulfill his purposes without destroying their free agency. A man may say, that he cannot see *how* the two things are consistent; and this may be true; for he cannot see how God operates on the mind. But his ignorance does not authorize him to affirm, that they are not consistent.

II. It is objected, that this doctrine makes God the author of sin. This objection has already been substantially answered. It is based upon the objection just refuted, that the doctrine of Divine Decrees is destructive of man's free agency. But if, as we have proved, the doctrine leaves man's free agency untouched, it is clear that his accountability is perfect, and he is the exclusive author of his own sins. Let the explanation of the doctrine already given, be kept in view. God, for wise reasons, was pleased to *permit* our first parents to be tempted and to fall. This permission, it is most evident, did not make him the author of their sin. He chose to overrule this sin to his own holy ends. This overruling of the sin which he permitted, certainly did not make him the author of the sin. God permitted Joseph's brethren to hate him and to sell him. This permission did not make him the author of that hatred, or of their act in selling him. God purposed to overrule their wickedness for good. The fact that he brought good out of their intended evil, did not make him the author of their evil. God decreed that Cyrus should take Babylon; but since he only permitted and controlled the unhallowed ambition of Cyrus, he did not thereby become the author of the sins committed by Cyrus. He decreed the crucifixion of Jesus Christ, and he permitted and overruled for good the wrath of the Jews against him. But he was not the author of the sin committed by them in crucifying Christ. The objection is founded upon an entirely false view of the doctrine, viz: that the Divine Decree is the *necessitating cause of sin,* or of the sinful acts of men. It is perfectly refuted, therefore, by simply giving a correct statement of the doctrine.

PART II.

DOCTRINE OF ELECTION.

DOCTRINE OF ELECTION.

CHAPTER I.

THE DOCTRINE OF ELECTION STATED.

THE doctrine of Election forms a distinct branch of the general doctrine of Divine Decrees. That we may determine whether it is Scriptural, it is particularly important that it be correctly stated. The most plausible objections urged against it, it is believed, derive all their apparent strength from the misapprehension or misrepresentation of it.

1. The doctrine of Election contemplates the whole human family as fallen in Adam, as by nature totally depraved, and justly exposed to eternal punishment. Now, if such is not the condition of men,—if they are not fallen, wholly depraved, and exposed to the just penalty of God's law, the doctrine is of course false. Consequently it has been denied and denounced by all who reject the doctrine of *Original Sin,* and deny that men "are by nature children of wrath."

2. The doctrine teaches, that God, for the glory of his name, purposed from eternity to renew, justify, sanctify, and save, through Jesus Christ, a multitude of the

human race, and to pass by others, leaving them the willing slaves of sin, and to punish them for their sin. The atonement made by Jesus Christ is indeed of infinite value, because made by a Being of infinite dignity, and is therefore sufficient for the salvation of all men; so that if God had purposed to save all, no change in the atonement, or addition to it, would have been necessary. Salvation is freely offered through Jesus Christ to all who hear the gospel; and all, being free moral agents, are free to accept or reject it. Depravity, though it renders men averse to the service of God and the gospel of Christ, does not interfere with their freedom of choice and their just accountability. All men, though free to accept or reject the offered salvation, will certainly reject it, if left to themselves; that is, if their hearts be not changed by the Holy Spirit. God, for his own glory, purposed to dispose a multitude to accept it by trusting in Christ. God had the best reasons for choosing the individuals whom he did choose, and for passing by others; but those reasons he has not made known. He has taught only, that the elect were not chosen because they were better than others. We, therefore, can only say:—"Even so, Father, for so it seemed good in thy sight." If it be asked, Why did not God determine to treat all alike, to bestow upon all equal privileges and blessings? we answer, we do not know. We know only, that, for wise reasons not revealed to men, he has given to some blessings to which they had no claim,—thus making them great debtors to his *grace;* and has withheld from others, gifts he was under no obligation to bestow.

Such is the doctrine of Election, with the explanations and qualifications given by Calvinists. Such is the doctrine as held by the Presbyterian Church. Is it true? Is it scriptural?

This is a subject in the examination of which we cannot safely rely either upon our feelings or upon unassisted reason. So far as we are able to reason on the subject of man's condition, it would appear to us more in accordance with the Divine perfections to have preserved our world free from sin and suffering. Some, indeed, have asserted that God *could not* do this, if he created free moral agents; but God has nowhere authorized such an assertion. And beside, it would seem to us far less difficult to preserve holy beings in a state of purity, than to restore them to holiness when they have become the willing slaves of sin, and have long indulged in the commission of it. If God could do the latter without interfering with the liberty of men, as it is admitted he does in a multitude of instances, who can deny that he might have done the former? Beside, if the free moral agency of holy beings necessarily exposes them to fall into sin, there can be no certainty that those redeemed by the blood of Christ will not sin even in heaven, and then be hurled, as were the fallen angels, down to hell. Now, although some professing Christians have held, that persons really regenerated might fall from grace in the present life; none, so far as we know, have held that such a thing might occur in heaven. The permission of sin must be regarded as a profound mystery, which, in this life, we may not comprehend. Nor is this the only mystery connected with the present condition of our race.

One is born blind, another is blessed with sight. One is born with a vigorous constitution, and enjoys almost uninterrupted health; another inherits a painful and incurable disease, and sinks early into the grave. One is born to wealth; another to poverty and want. One is born of infidel, or dissipated parents; another of parents who instill into the infant mind virtuous principles both by precept and example. One is born in the midst of pagan or papal darkness; another under the clear light of the gospel. These are differences deeply affecting the happiness of those concerned, yet depending not at all upon their character or conduct. Why are such differences permitted to exist? Doubtless God has wise reasons for his providential dealings; but to men they are profoundly mysterious. Indeed, the whole history of the world is a practical commentary upon the language of God by Isaiah:—"For my thoughts are not your thoughts, neither are your ways my ways, saith the Lord. For as the heavens are higher than the earth, so are my ways higher than your ways, and my thoughts than your thoughts."* And often, as we contemplate the high mysteries of God's dealings with men, we are constrained to adopt the language of Paul, while considering the rejection and dispersion of the Jews:—"O the depth of the riches both of the wisdom and knowledge of God! how unsearchable are his judgments, and his ways past finding out."† Our true position, in the investigation of a subject like the one before us, is that of *disciples*, sitting at the feet of Jesus to learn of him; and

* Isai. 55: 8, 9. † Rom. 11: 33.

our appropriate business is that of *interpreting the word of God,* not abstract reasoning, such as proud philosphers are wont to adopt. If any are disposed to reject the doctrine of Election without a prayerful and candid examination of its claims, let them not forget that it has commanded the firm belief of multitudes of the wisest and best men that have lived. There must, therefore, be strong reasons in favor of its truth.

CHAPTER II.

Objections to the Doctrine of Election stated, and the Errors and Inconsistencies of Arminianism exposed.

A number of general objections are urged against the doctrine of Election, which it will be satisfactory to consider before we proceed to the direct proof of its truth.

One of the most plausible objections is, *that the doctrine is inconsistent with the* JUSTICE *of God.* Now that God is infinitely just, we admit and assert; and if the doctrine of Election is indeed inconsistent with Divine justice, it must be rejected as false and injurious. Justice consists in a strict regard for all the rights or just claims of others. *Injustice,* in the Divine administration would necessarily consist, therefore, either in withholding from his creatures those blessings to which they have a just claim; or in inflicting upon them sufferings which they do not deserve. Does the doctrine of Election represent God as doing either of these things? If it does, the objection urged against it is valid; if it does not, the objection has no force. In what, then, consists the alleged injustice implied in the doctrine under consideration? It of course does not consist in the saving of the elect. Their salvation is indeed wholly of *grace;* but in the plan of salvation, the exercise of grace, it is admitted, is perfectly consistent with Divine justice,—its claims having been fully satisfied by Jesus Christ for his people. The injustice implied in the doctrine must, therefore, if it exist at all, be exercised toward the *non-elect.* Let us, then, carefully examine wherein, if this doctrine be true, they are treated unjustly. Are blessings withheld from them to which they have just claim? Or are sufferings inflicted which they do not merit? That we may satisfactorily answer these questions, let us get a distinct view of the real condition of the human race.

On the following points, the more evangelical class of Arminians agree with us: 1. That God created man in his moral image, in true holiness. 2. That our first parents yielded to the temptation of the devil, and fell from their original holiness. 3. That in his trial Adam was the *federal head* of his posterity, and that his first sin was imputed to them; and, consequently, they are regarded and treated as if they had done what he did. Of the consequences of the imputation of Adam's sin to his posterity, the Rev. Richard Watson says:—"The first consequence, then, of this imputation is the death of the body, to which all the descendants of Adam are made liable, and that on account of the sin of Adam." The *second* consequence, he says, is "death *spiritual,* that moral state which arises from the withdrawment of that intercourse of God with the human soul, in consequence of its becoming polluted, and of that influence upon it which is the only source and spring of the right and vigorous direction and employment of its powers in which its rectitude consists; a *deprivation* from which a *depravation* consequently and necessarily follows." The *third* consequence, according to the same author, "is *eternal death,* separation from God, and endless banishment from his glory in a future state."* Now, admitting the views of Mr. Watson concerning the imputation of Adam's sin, and the consequences flowing therefrom, to be correct, what is the real condition of the human family, aside from the plan of salvation? All are mortal, exposed to temporal death; all are spiritually dead, totally depraved; and all are "children of wrath," exposed to eternal misery. The doctrine of Election teaches, that God, of his infinite mercy, purposed, from eternity, to renew, sanctify, justify, and save, through Jesus Christ, a portion of the fallen race of Adam; and this doctrine, we are assured, is inconsistent with the justice of God. That is, if God should thus choose a portion of the human race, and pass by the remainder, leaving them in their fallen and condemned condition, he would thus do injustice to these last. Of course, as before remarked, he would, if the objection be well founded, either withhold from them what they have a just claim to, or inflict upon them sufferings they do not deserve.

Now, let us suppose, that God had passed by the whole human race, leaving them in their fallen, depraved, and condemned condition, as he passed by the fallen angels, would he have been chargeable with injustice toward them? If not, he would simply have left them to a just doom, and to a just punishment. But if he might justly pass by *all*, how is he chargeable with injustice toward those whom he does thus pass by? Does the injustice consist in saving some? Will it be

* Theol. Inst., pt. 2, ch. 18.

pretended, that his bestowing on some a *gracious* salvation, deprives others of what they had a just claim to? Those who are saved, receive blessings to which they have no claim,—are saved *by grace,* not by merit. Does the bestowing upon some men blessings to which they had no claim, give others a just claim to those blessings? If so, it would follow that but *one sinner* could be saved by grace; for so soon as saving grace was bestowed on one, all others would have a just claim to the same blessings, and would consequently receive them as *debt,* not as *grace.* But the idea is too absurd. If it be admitted that God might justly have passed by all men and left them to perish, it follows inevitably that in saving some he does no injustice to others whom he does not save. In other words, if God might justly leave all to perish, he is not in justice bound to save any; and if he is not bound to save any, he does no injustice to those whom he does not save.

If we can understand Mr. Watson, he contends that the imputation of Adam's sin to his posterity, and their consequent exposedness to eternal misery, are just. He says:—"The justice of this [i. e., their exposedness to eternal misery] is objected to, a point which will be immediately considered; but it is now sufficient to say, that if the making the descendants of Adam liable to eternal death, because of his offense, be unjust, the infliction of temporal death is so also,—the duration of the punishment making no difference in the simple question of justice. If punishment, whether of *loss* or of *pain,* be unjust, its measure and duration may be a greater or a less injustice; but it is unjust in every degree. If, then, we only confine the hurt we have received from Adam to bodily death,—if this legal result of his transgression only be imputed to us, and we are so constituted sinners as to become liable to it, we are in precisely the same difficulty, as to the equity of the proceedings, as when the legal result is extended further. The only way out of this dilemma is that adopted by Dr. Taylor, to consider death not as a punishment, but as a blessing, which involves the absurdity of making Deity threaten a benefit as a *penalty* for an offense, which sufficiently refutes the notion."* This language is sufficiently plain. Mr. Watson proves conclusively, that the imputation of Adam's sin to his posterity, together with all the consequences even to eternal misery, is strictly just. Most assuredly, then, it cannot be unjust in God to inflict upon any of his creatures *just punishment*. To assert that it is, would be a palpable contradiction.

But it may be said, that it would have been unjust in God to have passed by all the human race, and left them to perish in their sin; that since Adam's posterity had no agency in his sin by which they were brought into a ruined condition, God was bound to provide for them a way of escape. On this point the language of Mr. Watson appears contradictory. Speaking of natural death as coming upon Adam's posterity because of his sin, he says, "here was justice, the end of which is to support law, as that supports government." Of their spiritual death, flowing from the same cause, he says, "here was justice, a display of the evil of sin, and of the penalty it ever immediately induces. In regard to

* Theol. Inst., pt. 2, ch. 18.

the resurrection by Jesus Christ, regeneration by the Holy Spirit, and the offer of eternal life, he says, "*here is mercy.*" Now if such language means anything, it means that the justice of God would consign the whole human race to death,—temporal, spiritual, and eternal; and that it is *mercy* which affords them the offer of salvation. And yet he says immediately afterward: "In all this, it is impossible to impeach the equity of the Divine procedure, since no man suffers any loss or injury ultimately by the sin of Adam, but by his own willful obstinacy, — the 'abounding grace' by Christ Jesus, having placed before all men, upon their believing, not merely compensation for the loss and injury sustained by Adam, but infinitely higher blessings, both in kind and degree, than were forfeited in him." He here defends the justice of God in the imputation of Adam's sin, on the ground that by the plan of salvation through Jesus Christ he offers the human race the opportunity of escaping from the consequences of that imputation,—evidently implying, that but for the offer of salvation, which he yet ascribes to *mercy*, that imputation would be unjust. This ground is much more strongly taken, when he urges against the doctrine of Election the objection that it is unjust. He says:—"In whatever light the subject be viewed, no fault, in any right construction, can be chargeable upon the persons so punished, or as we may rather say, *destroyed;* since punishment supposes a judicial proceeding, which this act shuts out. For either the reprobates are destroyed for a pure reason of sovereignty, without any reference to their sinfulness, and thus all criminality is left out of the consideration; or they are destroyed for the sin of Adam, to which they were not consenting; or for personal faults resulting from a corruption of nature which they brought into the world with them, and which God wills not to correct, and they have no power to correct themselves. Every received notion of justice is thus violated." The position is here distinctly taken, that it would be unjust in God to pass by all or any of the human family, leaving them to perish in their sin, without both offering them a Saviour, and giving them such assistance that they can correct that corruption of nature with which they came into the world. Consequences of most serious import follow this position.

1. In the first place, it clearly charges God with *injustice.* Observe, Mr. Watson not only admits, but asserts that God did impute the sin of Adam to his posterity, and that the legitimate consequences of that imputation were natural death, spiritual death, and exposedness to eternal death; and yet he contends most earnestly, that it would be unjust that they should be left to suffer these consequences. Most certainly, then, the imputation itself, which exposes them to undeserved sufferings, is unjust. Nor is the difficulty at all removed by the fact, that God offers them the opportunity of salvation through Jesus Christ. An unjust act cannot be made just by another act intended to compensate for the injustice done. If I, without provocation, push a man into a pit, and he be badly bruised, it is no justification of the act that I let down a ladder for him, and call in a physician to cure his wounds. If the imputation of the sin of Adam to his posterity, with all the consequences legitimately flowing from it, be not in itself just, the provisions of the gospel, of which many

never hear, cannot make it so. These provisions can be considered in no other light, than as being *some amends* made for an injury previously done.

In a word, the human race are in their present lost condition, either by the operation of just principles or of unjust principles. If the former be admitted, then evidently there can be no injustice in their being left where justice placed them. If the latter be alleged, then God is charged with injustice. So far, then, from our doctrine being chargeable with making God unjust, the objection lies strongly against Arminianism!

2. The objection we are considering destroys all *grace* in the gospel system, and makes the salvation of men a mere matter of *debt*. As a matter of fact, the human race, it is admitted, are fallen, mortal, depraved, and exposed to eternal misery. If left in this condition, they must perish. But Mr. Watson and his Arminian brethren say, it would be most unjust that they should be left to perish. *Justice*, then, requires that an adequate provision be made for their escape. The gospel is such a provision. Is it not, then, clear that the mission of the Son of God into our world, his crucifixion, and the whole plan of salvation, is a mere matter of *justice* toward men,—a provision which God, who imputed to them Adam's sin, and thus brought them into their lost condition, was bound in justice to make? Observe, if Christ had not come into the world and died, all men must have perished. But, says Mr. Watson, they would be destroyed "for a pure reason of sovereignty, without any reference to their sinfulness, and thus all criminality is left out of the consideration; or they are destroyed for the sin of Adam, to which they

were not consenting; or for personal faults resulting from a corruption of nature which they brought into the world with them, and which God wills not to correct, and they have no power to correct themselves. Every received notion of justice is thus violated." Evidently, according to this reasoning, God was bound to send his Son to die for man, to offer them salvation, and give them sufficient aid to enable them to accept. And if, when the offer is made, any accept it, God is bound in justice to save them; for surely it would be unjust that any one perish who accepts the offer of life which God was bound to make. And, then, it is not only true that all dying in infancy are saved (which we believe), but both they and believing adults are saved, not by grace, but by *justice*. It would have been unjust that either class should perish.

Indeed, if the principles advanced by Mr. Watson are true, we see no necessity for an atonement. If *justice* requires that men should have the offer of salvation, why should Christ suffer to make it consistent for God to do a just thing? Then indeed *the law*, which is just, would offer salvation without an atonement. Where, then, is the *grace* in the plan of salvation? There can be none.

How different this view from that presented in the Scriptures:—" God so loved the world, that he gave his only begotten Son, that whosoever believeth in him, might not perish, but have everlasting life." Men were in a perishing condition, and the offer of salvation through Christ is here declared to be the result of *boundless love*, not of Divine justice toward men. Accordingly Paul says:—" Ye know *the grace* of our Lord Jesus Christ, that though he was rich, yet for your sakes he became poor, that ye through his poverty might be rich."*—The whole provision and the entire salvation of man is declared to be the manifestation of the boundless grace of God, not in any degree the result of Divine justice to injured man. "For by grace are ye saved through faith: and that not of yourselves; it is the gift of God." "The WAGES of sin is death; but the GIFT of God is eternal life through Jesus Christ our Lord."

We are constrained to charge upon Arminianism, that it destroys all grace in the plan of redemption. Is there grace in the salvation of infants? No; for it is alleged that it would be most unjust that they should perish because of their connection with Adam, and of their consequent depravity. *Justice*, therefore, saves them. Is there grace in the salvation of adults? No; for they derive their natural death and their depravity, from which flow all their sins, from Adam; and God is bound to offer them deliverance, and, of course, to save them, if they accept the offer.

3. There is another most serious error in the doctrine of Mr. Watson. He evidently considers depravity of heart as so far destroying or impairing the free agency and accountability of man, that unless divine influence be exerted upon them to remove its effects, they cannot be justly required to repent and turn from their sins, and to trust in Jesus Christ. He says:—"If all men everywhere would condemn it, as most contrary to justice and right, that a sovereign should condemn to death one or more of his subjects for not obeying laws which it is absolutely impossible for them under any circumstances

---

* 2 Cor., 8, 9.

which they can possibly avail themselves of to obey, and much more the greater part of his subjects, and to require them, on pain of aggravated punishment, to do something in order to the pardon and remission of their offenses, which he knows they cannot do, say to stop the tide or to remove a mountain, it implies a charge as awfully and obviously unjust against God, to suppose him to act precisely in the same manner as to those whom he has passed by and rejected, without any avoidable fault of their own." In the same connection he speaks of "personal faults resulting from a corruption of nature which they brought into the world with them, and which God wills not to correct, and they have no power to correct themselves," and represents the non-elect as "left under a necessity of sinning in every condition." Now if this representation be correct, the effect of depravity upon the minds of men is so completely to paralyze their powers, that they are under a *necessity* of sinning, and can no more love and obey God than they can stop the tide or remove a mountain. Look at the consequences which necessarily flow from such a principle.

1. Men left without divine influence to relieve them from the effects of depravity are not accountable beings, and are under no obligation to obey the law of God. If they can no more obey the law of God than they can stop the tide, and are under a necessity of sinning, they can be under no obligation to obey. And if they are under no obligation to obey, they are not chargeable with sin in disobeying; and if not chargeable with sin in disobeying, they do not and cannot sin. The conclusion, therefore, to which we are forced, according to Mr. Watson's doctrine, is that men, left in their natural state,

are so depraved that they cannot sin! for certain it is, that they who cannot obey, cannot disobey.

2. According to this doctrine, the very first effect of Divine grace on the hearts of men, is to enable them to sin! Left entirely to themselves, as we have seen, they could not sin; but it is admitted that all do sin when they reach the period of moral agency, which they could not do if left without divine influence. Does it not follow, that all the actual transgressions of men, so far as they possess any criminality, are traceable to that divine influence which, according to our Arminian brethren, is given to every man? And does not this look like making God the author of sin?

3. According to the doctrine we are considering, the more depraved men become the less sin they commit! Total depravity, we are assured, makes it *necessary* for men to sin. Now let the sinner reject that divine aid which is proffered him, extinguish by his persevering wickedness that spark of grace which it is said God has put into his heart, and ever after he is under a necessity of doing as he does,—can no more obey God than he can stop the tide. He may be criminal, to some extent, in extinguishing that spark, just as a man would be in deliberately putting out his eyes; but as the latter would be under no obligation to see after his eyes were put out, so the former would be under no obligation to obey God after he had extinguished the spark of grace in his heart. Forever afterward he would be incapable of either obeying or disobeying God. He could sin no more!

4. If the effect of depravity be to destroy free agency and accountability, then the more depraved a man be-

comes, even though he have not entirely expelled from his heart all divine influence, the less capable he is of sinning. So that the most depraved men in the world really commit less sin than those who are far better!

5. According to this doctrine, the devils and all lost spirits are wholly incapable of sinning; for most assuredly they are totally depraved, and have in their hearts not a spark of Divine grace. They devise wicked plans, and execute them; and they blaspheme the name of God; but since they are under a *necessity* of doing those things, and can be under no obligation to do otherwise, they are chargeable with nothing criminal. They are so deeply depraved, that they cannot sin! To such absurdities does the doctrine lead, upon which is founded the charge of injustice against the doctrine of Election.

The plain truth is, that there is no tendency in depravity to destroy or impair man's free agency and just accountability. Satan has free agency as perfect now, as before he fell from heaven. The only difference is that he loved to do right then, and he loves to do wrong now. But in choosing to gratify his evil affections by doing wrong now, he is as free as he was in choosing to gratify his pure affections by doing right then; and, therefore, he is under the same obligation to obey God now as then. The evidence of our free agency is our own consciousness, and the worst man is as distinctly conscious of acting freely, and of being justly accountable, as the best. It is not true, therefore, that the sinner, left to himself, is under the necessity of sinning; nor is it true, that to require him to obey God, or to believe in Christ, would be as unreasonable and as unjust as to require him to stop the tide or to remove a mountain. The charge of injustice against the doctrine of Election, is made out by connecting Arminian philosophy with Calvinistic theology. We protest against the unnatural union, and against all inferences drawn from it. We hold, that the human mind is from its very nature free, and must always continue free; and consequently the obligation of all men capable of understanding the requirements of the Divine law to obey it, is perfect, whether they are totally depraved or not. That there is a sense in which the sinner *cannot* serve God, is true; but his inability is not of a kind which interferes with his free agency and accountability. Like Joseph's brethren, who "hated him and *could not* speak peaceably to him," the sinner is the more criminal for his inability.

To sum up the whole matter, the human race are in their lost and ruined condition by the operation of just principles, or they are not. If they are, God might justly leave them in that condition; and if, for reasons satisfactory to Infinite Wisdom, he should pass by some of them, there would be no injustice done them. He would withhold nothing from them to which they have any just claim, and he would inflict on them no punishment they do not deserve. For it is absurd to say, that men are *justly* exposed to eternal misery; and yet it would be *unjust* that they should suffer it. It is the same as saying, it is unjust to inflict a just penalty.

But if it be alleged, that men are fallen and exposed to ruin by the operation of principles that are not just, then, in the first place, it follows that the principles of God's moral government, under which he placed Adam and his posterity, are unjust; and, in the second place, that there is no *grace* in his remedial system,—it being nothing more than God's plan of offering to men what in justice he could not withhold.

We feel constrained here distinctly to charge, not upon Arminians themselves, but upon their system, that it impugns the principles of God's moral government, by admitting the *fact* of the imputation of Adam's sin to his posterity, and yet declaring the legitimate consequences of that imputation *unjust.* We charge that system with making the whole plan of salvation a matter not of *grace* but of *debt,* by holding God under obligation to provide men the means of escape from their fallen condition.

Whatever difficulties men may find in seeing the consistency of the imputation of Adam's sin to his posterity with the principles of justice, so long as we admit the fact (and the Scriptures do plainly teach it), we must believe it perfectly consistent. It is certain that God never adopted an unjust principle,—a principle which, legitimately acted upon, would do injustice to any of his creatures. If, therefore, he did adopt the principle of federal representation, as Arminians admit, that principle is just, whether with our present limited knowledge we can see it to be so or not. There is, however, really no more difficulty in reconciling with justice the imputation of Adam's sin to his posterity, than in reconciling the sufferings of infants and universal depravity, or the fact that children do, in multitudes of instances, suffer terribly in consequence of the wickedness of their parents. Indeed it would not be difficult to prove that the doctrine of the Scriptures on this point, is attended with fewer difficulties than any theory by which men have attempted to explain the existing state of things.

If, then, the doctrine of imputation is just, and if men are free agents irrespective of any divine influence upon their hearts, the doctrine of Election is not inconsistent with the justice of God. The non-elect are deprived of nothing to which they have just claim, and are subjected to no unmerited punishment. They loved sin, and God left them to pursue the course they chose. Indeed multitudes of them are chargeable with freely and deliberately rejecting the offers of salvation. The opposers of this doctrine, then, must assail it on some other ground.

A second objection to the doctrine of Election is, *that it represents God as* A RESPECTER OF PERSONS. Now, we cheerfully admit that the objection, if well founded, is fatal to the doctrine; for it is certain, as the Scriptures repeatedly declare, that God is not a respecter of persons. Before we can determine what force there is in the objection, we must ascertain the precise meaning of the phrase *respecter of persons*. This we can do by comparing the passages of Scripture in which it occurs. Moses charged the Jewish judges:—"Ye shall not respect persons in judgment; ye shall hear the small as well as the great; but ye shall not be afraid of the face of man," etc. Again:—"Thou shalt not wrest judgment; thou shalt not respect persons, neither take a gift; for a gift doth blind the eyes of the wise, and pervert the words of the righteous." In these passages, it is evident that the phrase has reference exclusively to the conduct of a *judge* trying a cause brought legally before him. If in his decisions he were influenced not by the law and the testimony, but by personal prejudice in favor of one of the parties, or by the fear of man, or by a bribe, he would be a respecter of persons. In the same sense it is applied to God: "For the Lord your God is God of gods, and Lord of lords, a great God, a mighty, and a terrible, which regardeth not persons, nor taketh reward: he doth execute the judgment of the fatherless and widow, and loveth the stranger, in giving him food and raiment." Paul explains the phrase, when he says, God "will render to every man according to his deeds, etc.: for there is no respect of persons with God." When Peter saw that God had accepted Cornelius, a pious Gentile, he said:—"Of a truth I perceive that God is no respecter of persons: but in every nation he that feareth him and worketh righteousness, is accepted with him."* If God had rejected Cornelius, who was a truly pious man, simply because he was a Gentile, while he would receive a Jew of the same character, he would have been a respecter of persons. But inasmuch as he accepts all righteous men, of whatever nation, he is not so. A respecter of persons, then, is one who, acting as a judge, decides not according to law and testimony, but is governed by sinister motives; who does not treat those who come before him according to their *character;* who withholds from some that to which they have just claim, in order to give to others what is not their due; or who is governed in his treatment of men by prejudice, not by a proper estimate of their real character. Precisely

* Acts 10: 34, 35.

this interpretation of the phrase *respecter of persons*, is given by Dr. Adam Clarke.*

Now the doctrine of Election teaches that all the human race are fallen, depraved, and exposed to the wrath of God, none of them having any claims upon God; and that upon some of them he, for his own glory, bestows gifts and blessings which he does not bestow upon others. Is this doctrine liable to the objection, that it makes God a respecter of persons? The objection is based upon the principle, that God is bound to give to every individual of the human family *precisely the same or equal gifts;* and, consequently, if in any one

* In his Commentary on Acts x. 34, he thus explains it; "He does not esteem a *Jew*, because he is a *Jew;* nor does he detest a *Gentile*, because he is a *Gentile*. It was a long and deeply-rooted opinion among the Jews, that God never would extend his favor to the Gentiles; and that the descendants of Jacob only should enjoy his peculiar favor and benediction. Of this opinion was St. Peter, previously to the heavenly vision mentioned in this chapter. He was now convinced that *God was no respecter of persons;* that all must stand before his judgment-seat, to be judged according to the deeds done in the body; so no one nation of people, or individual, could expect to find a more favorable decision than another, who was precisely in the *same* moral state: for the phrase *respect of persons*, is used in reference to *unjust decisions* in a *court of justice*, when through favor, or interest, or bribe, a culprit is acquitted, and a righteous or innocent person condemned. And as there is *no iniquity* (decisions contrary to equity) *with God*, so he could not shut out the pious *prayers*, sincere *fasting*, and benevolent *alms-giving* of Cornelius; because the very spring whence they proceeded was his own grace and mercy. Therefore he could not receive even a *Jew* into his favor (in preference to such a person), who had either abused his grace or made a less godly use of it than this Gentile had done."

instance he fails to do this, he is a respecter of persons Or if it be admitted that he may bestow upon some gifts which he grants not to others no more undeserving, those who press this objection must tell us precisely *how far* he may proceed in making a difference before he becomes chargeable with respecting persons. One individual, for example, is born blind, and another is blessed with vision. God in his providence bestows upon the latter an inestimable blessing, which he withholds from the former; and this difference, existing before either could do good or evil, is not founded on difference of character. Is God, then, a respecter of persons? The Arminian will agree with us that he is not. But why not? Mr. Watson urges against Election the objection under consideration on the ground that it makes the acceptance or rejection of men stand on some ground of aversion or dislike, which cannot be resolved into any *moral rule* and has no respect to the *merits of the case itself.** No; it represents God as bestowing upon some persons gifts which he bestows not on others who possess the same depravity of heart. And in the case we are considering, God certainly does withhold from one of his creatures a blessing of incalculable value, which he bestows upon another; and, as before remarked, this difference is made before either of them has done good or evil. Into what *moral rule* can we resolve this difference? What respect has it to *the merits of the case itself?* Yet all are compelled to admit that God does make just such differences, and even greater, in his treatment of his creatures in ten thousand instances;

* Theol. Inst., pt. 2, ch. 26.

and still he is not a respecter of persons. Why such differences are made, it is impossible for us to know; but certain it is, that God has the best reasons for making them.

But it may be said, that however it may be consistent in God to make a difference in the treatment of his creatures, as regards mere *temporal blessings,* such as vision, health, wealth, liberty, and the like, he cannot, without being a respecter of persons, make a similar difference in the bestowment of *spiritual blessings* connected with the salvation of the soul. We answer: 1. That it does not appear how the *principle* is changed, when the difference relates to spiritual gifts. If God may withhold from an individual the blessing of *vision,* why not any other blessing? The withholding of a greater blessing might be a greater injustice, if there were injustice in the case, or a more glaring manifestation of respect of persons; but the *principle* is the same. 2. But Mr. Watson, even when urging the objection against election, that it makes God a respecter of persons, concedes the principle which overthrows the objection. He says:—"This phrase, we grant, is not to be interpreted as though the bounties of the Almighty were dispensed in equal measures to his creatures. In the administration of favor, there is place for the exercise of that prerogative which, in a just sense, is called the sovereignty of God; but *justice* knows but one rule,"* etc. And are not *all* the blessings of salvation through Christ mere *favors* to men? Do not even Arminians hold that they are all of *grace?* If so, there is confessedly room for the exercise of sovereignty.

* Theol. Inst., pt. 2, ch. 26.

If men have just claim to any of these blessings, they are not *gracious.* If they are gracious, and men consequently have no claim to them, it is clear beyond dispute that no injustice is done by withholding them. So that what Mr. Watson says about *the one rule of justice,* does not apply to the case in hand.

But Mr. Watson admits that God may and does make a difference in the treatment of his creatures concerning even *spiritual blessings.* Among the benefits derived to man from the Atonement, he mentions the revelation of the will of God, and the declaration of his purposes of grace as to man's actual redemption. "*These purposes,*" he remarks, "*have been declared to man with great inequality we grant, a mystery which we are not able to explain,*"* *etc.* Again he says:—"The second kind of Election which we find in Scripture is the election of nations or bodies of people to eminent religious privileges, and in order to accomplish, by their superior illumination, the merciful purposes of God, in benefiting other nations or bodies of people. Thus the descendants of Abraham, the Jews, were *chosen* to receive special revelations of truth, and to be 'the people of God,' to be his visible Church, and publicly to observe and uphold his worship." Again:—"For Christians were the subjects, also, of this second kind of Election,—the election of bodies of men to be the visible people and Church of God in the world, and to be endowed with peculiar privileges."† Now let us see how the objection lies. It is admitted, that God may make great differences in the bestowment of *temporal blessings* upon different nations and individuals,

* Theol. Inst., pt. 2, ch. 23. † Ibid., ch. 26.

without being a respecter of persons. It is also admitted, that he may and does choose some to peculiar *religious privileges*, of which others are left destitute,—privileges the design and tendency of which are to secure their conversion and salvation,—without being a respecter of persons. But it is asserted, that if he should go one step further, and exert upon some a *sanctifying influence* which he does not exert upon others, he would thereby make himself a respecter of persons! How, we ask, have our Arminian friends ascertained the precise amount of difference God may make in the bestowment of his grace, without becoming a respecter of persons? Their position is plainly contradictory. They admit the *principle* embraced in the doctrine of Election, viz: *that God makes a difference in the bestowment of his blessings upon men;* and then directly deny it, holding that to do so, would make him a respecter of persons!

Now the plain truth is, that *grace,* from its very nature, must be free; and, therefore, God may bestow or withhold it as in his infinite wisdom he chooses. And so long as he withholds from no one of his creatures anything to which he has a just claim, and inflicts upon no one more punishment than his sin deserves, and so long as he rejects no righteous man; no one has the right to find fault, or charge him with respecting persons. The doctrine of Election does not represent him as doing either of these things, and consequently the objection we are considering is of no force whatever.

A third objection to the doctrine of Election is, that it is inconsistent with the *sincerity* of God in offering salvation by Christ to all who hear the gospel. But if, as we believe, every man is a free moral agent, perfectly free to accept or reject the offer of salvation, where is the insincerity in making the offer to all? It is objected again, that according to the Calvinistic view, Christ made no atonement for the non-elect; and our Arminian friends have urged against the doctrine all those passages of Scripture which represent Christ as having *died for all men.* But the word *for,* like all other prepositions, has a number of meanings. What, then, do they mean by affirming that Christ died *for* all men? Do they mean that he made an atonement which, in consequence of his infinite dignity, is *sufficient* for all men? If so, we have no controversy with them; for we hold that the Atonement is of infinite value, and that no one is lost because its virtue is exhausted. Do they mean that in making an atonement Christ designed *to offer salvation* indiscriminately to all men? If so, we agree with them. Our views of the gospel require us to preach it "to every creature." Do they mean that Christ really purposed *to save* all men by his death? They cannot mean this; for, in the first place, multitudes were forever lost before he died, and it will scarcely be pretended that he designed to save them. In the second place, he certainly knew who would believe and be saved; for he knew all things; and it would be absurd to say that he designed to save those he knew he never would save. What, then, we again ask, do Arminians mean by the declaration that Christ died *for* all men? Do they mean that he really intended to save *no one individual,* but to offer salvation alike to all, and to give all equal opportunities to accept it? They cannot mean this; for, in the first place, it is an undeniable fact that Christ has not made the offer of salvation to all. Multitudes have lived and died without ever so much as hearing his name. If it be said, the heathen are responsible only for the light they have, we cheerfully admit it; but they are deeply depraved and under condemnation, and the question is not whether they will be chargeable with the additional sin of rejecting the gospel, but whether they have light and divine influence enough to save them without the gospel. If it be said that the heathen are *all* saved without means, then are they in a better condition than if they had the gospel, and it would be cruel to send it to them.

In the second place, it is certain that God has not given to all equal opportunities of being saved. For of those who have heard the gospel, some have far better opportunities of being instructed in its glorious truths, and are placed under much stronger influences of a religious character than others. We are well satisfied, that if Arminians, by asserting that Christ died *for* all men, mean anything more than that he designed to offer salvation indiscriminately to all who hear the gospel, they will find it difficult to tell what they do mean. The atonement, we believe, is sufficient to save all, if they would believe; all are free moral agents, and may accept or refuse the offer of life. The gospel may, therefore, be sincerely offered to all, while they may be left to their own choice.

It is true, God does not subdue their pride, their enmity, their unbelief, and their love of sin; but will it be pretended that God cannot sincerely offer salvation to a free moral agent, unless, in addition to the invitation, he by a special influence dispose him to accept of it? God invites them to come to Christ. They are unwilling to come, and he lets them alone,—leaves them to their own inclinations. This is all. If it be said, God knows that without the special influences of his Spirit sinners will not come; we answer, that according to the admission of Mr. Watson, he knows who will accept and who will reject the offer of salvation; and yet this knowledge is admitted to be perfectly consistent with sincerity in inviting those who, he knows, will not come.

A fourth objection to the doctrine of Election is, that it involves in it the *damnation of infants.* The following language of the Westminster Confession is appealed to in proof of the objection:—"Elect infants, dying in infancy, are regenerated and saved by Christ through the Spirit, who worketh when, and where, and how he pleaseth." On this point we remark: It is certain that Presbyterians have never understood this language as teaching the doctrine of infant damnation. Persons have often asserted that they had heard the doctrine preached, but on particular inquiry it has been found that their statements were either maliciously false, or mere *inferences* of their own from what the preacher said. But no respectable Presbyterian writer can be found, either in ancient or modern times, who has taught that any dying in infancy are lost. Calvinistic writers, it is true, hold that the sin of Adam was imputed to his posterity, he being their federal head, and that they consequently are involved with him in a common condemnation; and the more evangelical Arminians, as we have seen, hold the same doctrine. Calvinists, therefore, believe that infants as well as adults are exposed to eternal death, and are saved only *by grace* through Christ Jesus. But no respectable Presbyterian writer, we repeat, can be found who teaches that any dying in infancy are actually lost. The doctrine of Infant damnation was charged upon the Presbyterian Church by Alexander Campbell, in a public debate with the author of these pages. In reply we said :—"I am truly gratified that the gentleman has brought forward the charge against us, of holding the doctrine of the damnation of infants; because it is believed by many who are unacquainted with our views. He says, our Confession of Faith teaches this doctrine. This is not correct. It is true that it speaks of elect infants,—'Elect infants dying in infancy, are regenerated and saved by Christ through the Spirit.' Are all infants, dying in infancy, elect? All Presbyterians who express an opinion on the subject, so believe. The expression, 'elect infants,' the gentleman seems to think, implies non-elect infants; but I call upon him to produce one respectable Presbyterian author who has expressed the opinion that infants dying in infancy are lost. Mr. Campbell boasts of his familiarity with the doctrines of our Church. He, then, is the very man to make good this oft-repeated charge. I call for the proof. So far as I know the sentiments of Presbyterians on this subject, they believe that all that die in infancy are of the elect,—are chosen of God to eternal life, and are sanctified by the Holy Spirit and saved according to his eternal purpose. Infants do not die by accident. He whose providence extends to the falling of a sparrow, takes care of every human being; and we believe that his purpose is to save those whom he calls from time before they are capable of knowing the truth. But the gentleman has made the charge that the Presbyterian Church holds the doctrine of the damnation of infants, and now I demand the proof." In answer to this demand, repeatedly made, Mr. Campbell quoted one or two passages from the writings of Calvin, and one from Turretine, in which those great and good men opposed the doctrine of the Pelagians and Socinians, who hold that Adam's sin did not affect his posterity, and that men are not born in original sin ; and in which they affirmed that all Adam's posterity are exposed to eternal death, and might justly have been left to perish. But neither of them taught that any infant is in fact lost. They simply taught, that the salvation of all, infants as well as adults, is of *grace,* not of *justice.*

We state these facts to show that the fairest opportunity was given to a man well qualified to prove the charge true, that Presbyterians hold the doctrine of infant damnation; that although both our challenge and our explanation of Presbyterian faith have been extensively circulated, the former has not even yet been met, while the latter has been universally approved by Presbyterians. If, then, Presbyterians are capable of understanding the language of their own Creed, it does not, directly or impliedly, teach the doctrine of infant damnation. And until it can be shown that God could not predestinate to eternal life all those he is pleased to call from earth in infancy, the objection we are considering is of no weight whatever.

We have now carefully examined the most plausible objections urged against the doctrine of Election, and we think they have been proved to be unfounded. We now proceed to the direct inquiry, whether this doctrine is taught in the sacred Scriptures.

CHAPTER III.

THE DOCTRINE OF ELECTION PROVED FROM THE WORD OF GOD.

Is the doctrine of Election, as we have stated it, taught in the Scriptures? This, after all, is the great question. We propose to prove it true by clear Scripture testimony.

I. *God is the author of regeneration.* Every true Christian has experienced a great moral change, commonly called regeneration, the new birth, the new creation, etc.; and of this change God is the author. Happily the more evangelical class of Arminians, agree with us here. John Wesley defines regeneration or the new birth, in the following language:—"It is that great change which God works in the soul, when he brings it into life; when he raises it from the death of sin to the life of righteousness. It is the change wrought in the whole soul by the Almighty spirit of God, when it is 'created anew in Christ Jesus,' when it is 'renewed after the image of God in righteousness and true holiness,' when the love of the world is changed into the love of God; pride into humility; passion into meekness," etc. The Rev. Richard Watson thus defines regeneration: "It is that mighty change in man, wrought by the Holy Spirit, by which the dominion which sin has over him in his natural state, and which he deplores and struggles against in his peniten state, is broken and abolished, so that, with full choice of will, and the energy of right affections, he serves God freely, and runs in the way of his commandments."

But we need not the admission of Arminians on this point; for both the Bible and the experience of believers do clearly teach that regeneration is the work of God, not of man. They who receive Christ, are "born, not of blood, nor of the will of the flesh, nor of the will of man, but of God."* Of this same work Paul says: "God, even when we were dead in sins, hath quickened us together with Christ." And again: "For we are his workmanship created in Christ Jesus unto good works, which God hath before ordained that we should walk in them."† A multitude of passages of Scripture might be adduced in proof of this truth, but it is unnecessary.

II. *God does this work in fulfillment of* HIS PURPOSES. When he regenerates the heart of a sinner, he does it not *accidentally*, but *designedly;* and the design or purpose was formed before the act was done. Therefore Paul ascribes it to the love of God. "But God, who is rich in mercy, for his great love wherewith he loved us, even when we were dead in sins, hath quickened us together with Christ." God loved us, and therefore he determined to quicken us. But this fact is too clear to require or admit proof.

III. *The purpose to regenerate particular individuals was not formed because God foresaw that they would be better than others, or that they would repent and believe in Christ, but of his own sovereign mercy.* The more evan-

---

* John 1: 13. † Eph. 2: 5. 8.

gelical class of Arminians agree with us "that man is by nature totally corrupt and degenerate, and of himself incapable of any good thing,"—that all are "born in a state of spiritual death."* John Wesley addresses the sinner in the following language:—"Know thyself to be a sinner, and what manner of sinner thou art. Know that corruption of thy inmost nature, whereby thou art very far gone from original righteousness, whereby 'the flesh lusteth' always 'contrary to the spirit,' through that 'carnal mind' which 'is enmity against God,' which 'is not subject to the law of God, neither indeed can be.' Know that thou art corrupted in every power, in every faculty of thy soul; that thou art totally corrupted in every one of these, all the foundations being out of course. The eyes of thine understanding are darkened, so that they cannot discern God, or the things of God. The clouds of ignorance and error rest upon thee, and cover thee with the shadow of death. Thou knowest nothing yet as thou oughtest to know, neither God, nor the world, nor thyself. Thy will is no longer the will of God, but is utterly perverse and distorted, averse from all good, from all which God loves, and prone to all evil, to every abomination which God hateth. Thy affections are alienated from God, and scattered abroad over all the earth. All thy passions, both thy desires and aversions, thy joys and sorrows, thy hopes and fears, are out of frame, are either undue in their degree, or placed on undue objects. So that there is no soundness in thy soul; but 'from the crown of the head to the sole of the feet' (to use the

* Watson's Theol. Inst., pt. 2, ch. 18.

strong expression of the prophet), there are only 'wounds, and bruises, and putrefying sores.' Such is the inbred corruption of thy heart, of thy very inmost nature. * * * * And what fruits can grow on such branches as these? Only such as are bitter and evil continually."* Again:—"And in Adam all died, all human kind, all the children of men who were then in Adam's loins. The natural consequence of this is, that every one descended from him comes into the world spiritually dead, dead to God, wholly dead in sin; entirely void of the life of God; void of the image of God, of all that righteousness and holiness wherein Adam was created. Instead of this, every man born into the world now bears the image of the devil, in pride and self-will; the image of the beast, in sensual appetites and desires. This, then, is the foundation of the new birth, — the entire corruption of our nature."†

Such is the strong language, not too strong, of Wesley concerning the total depravity of every human being in a state of nature. Now it is certain, that in beings of such moral character God sees nothing morally good, nothing of holiness; and consequently no one can be regenerated because of his being morally better than others. There is no real goodness in any human being before regeneration, and therefore God could not have purposed to regenerate any one because he foresaw that there would be in him more goodness or holiness than other sinners possess. Mr. Wesley himself maintains

---

* Sermon on the Way to the Kingdom.

† Sermon on New Birth.

that the new birth "is the *first point* of sanctification."* If there were any true holiness in any soul before regeneration, that soul would not be dead in sin, and therefore could not be *quickened* or made alive. It might become more holy, but it could not be *regenerated,* because regeneration is the beginning of holiness in the heart, and sanctification is the progress of the work begun in regeneration.

After reading the strong declarations of Methodist writers concerning the total depravity of all men by nature, and concerning the nature of regeneration, we cannot but be astonished to find them contending earnestly that sinners do exercise true repentance and saving faith before they are regenerated, and that God regenerates them because of their repentance and faith. This error (for such we must consider it), forms one of the most effective reasons for the rejection of the doctrine of Election, and for the practice of receiving unregenerate persons called *Seekers* into the Church.

Let us examine the question briefly. *Do sinners exercise true evangelical repentance and saving faith before they are regenerated?* What is the nature of repentance? That there is a kind of repentance exercised by unconverted men, we do not deny. Judas, when he saw that the Saviour, whom he had betrayed, was condemned, "repented himself, and brought again the thirty pieces of silver to the chief priests and elders, saying, I have sinned in that I have betrayed the innocent blood;" but the repentance of Judas was of no avail. It was the anguish caused by the lashings of a guilty conscience,

---

* Sermon on God's Vineyard.

and by the fearful looking for of the judgment of God. The worst men often have such repentance, and lost spirits never cease to feel it. It is a sorrow that "worketh death."

But true repentance is a *change of mind;* for such is the meaning of the Greek word *metanoia*, translated *repentance.* In the true penitent there is a change of *views*, and a corresponding change of *affections*. Sin appears in its true light, and is hated, deplored, confessed, and forsaken. The language of genuine repentance is: "Father, I have sinned against heaven and before thee, and am no more worthy to be called thy son: make me as one of thy hired servants."* The publican was a true penitent, when "standing afar off, he would not lift up so much as his eyes unto heaven, but smote upon his breast, saying, God be merciful to me a sinner."† Now, what is the moral character of this repentance? It certainly springs from correct views of human obligation and of sin against God. Sin is seen to be hateful, and is hated. Genuine sorrow is felt in view of sin committed against God. Humble confession is made, sin abandoned, and forgiveness sought. Are not such feelings morally right? Can a child give better evidence of affection for a father, than that he sincerely sorrows for his disobedience, confesses it, and returns to his duty? Does he not thus afford as strong evidence of filial affection, as when he is happy in the smiles of his father? Is it not true, that the more depraved men are, the less genuine repentance they feel for their sins?— And is it not equally true, that the more piety they have

---

* Luke 15: 18, 19.

† Luke 18: 13.

the more deeply they repent, when made sensible of having done wrong? Concerning the moral character of repentance, we must take one of three positions, viz: It possesses no moral character at all, and is consequently worthless; or it is bad, and therefore aggravates the condemnation of the penitent; or it is good. No one can believe, either that it is indifferent or bad; it is, therefore, perfectly clear that it is morally good. Hence God has made precious promises to the true penitent. "But to this man will I look, even to him that is poor and of a contrite spirit, and trembleth at my word."* "The sacrifices of God are a broken spirit; a broken and a contrite heart, O God, thou wilt not despise."† When Peter related to the Church at Jerusalem the circumstances attending the admission of Cornelius and his family to the Christian Church, "they held their peace, and glorified God, saying, Then hath God also to the Gentiles granted *repentance unto life*."‡

We come, then, to the conclusion, that repentance flows from love to God and hatred of sin,—that it is morally good,—that in the exercise of repentance, men render true obedience to God. Now, is it possible for a heart totally depraved, "dead in trespasses and sins," to exercise such repentance? If repentance is morally good, the heart that repents has something of moral goodness or holiness, and is therefore spiritually alive; for holiness is spiritual life, as depravity is spiritual death. Such a heart has been regenerated; and repentance, which is morally good, is one of the fruits of that change. For, as Mr. Wesley well declares, holiness

---

* Isai. 66: 2. † Ps. 51: 17. ‡ Acts 11: 18.

"cannot commence in the soul until that change be wrought,—until by the power of the Highest overshadowing us, we are 'brought from darkness to light, from the power of Satan unto God;' that is, until we are born again; which, therefore, is absolutely necessary in order to holiness."*

Let us place this argument in another light. True repentance flows from *love to God*. There can be but three causes of repentance. It may be merely the result of the lashings of a guilty conscience, or simple remorse; or it may arise from a guilty conscience and the dread of future punishment; or it may be chiefly from love to God. The repentance which flows from the two first-named causes, may be and often is experienced by the worst men, such as Judas Iscariot, and could in no degree contribute to the soul's salvation. It is not the repentance which God requires. But if true repentance flows from love to God, the penitent is regenerated; for "every one that loveth is born of God, and knoweth God."†

Again, repentance is pleasing to God; for it is obedience to his command, and life is promised on condition of it. But "they that are in the flesh cannot please God." All persons are either in the flesh or in the spirit; and Paul says:—"Ye are not in the flesh, but in the Spirit, if so be that the Spirit of God dwell in you."‡ All, therefore, are in the flesh who have not the Spirit of God dwelling in them,—who are unrenewed; and they cannot please God. The argument is clear and conclusive. They who are in the flesh (unregenerate),

---

* Sermon on New Birth, † 1 John 4 : 7. ‡ Rom. 8 : 8, 9

cannot please God. But true penitents do please him. Therefore true penitents are not unregenerate.

It is equally easy to prove that *saving faith* does not precede regeneration, but is one of its fruits. What is the nature of Christian faith? Is it a mere intellectual conviction of the truth? If it were, it would not differ materially from the faith of devils. But "with *the heart* man believeth unto righteousness."* True faith enlists the *affections* as well as the intellect; it "worketh by love." Mr. Wesley himself declares, that the faith through which we are saved, is distinguished from the faith of a devil by this, that "it is not barely a speculative, rational thing, a cold, lifeless assent, a train of ideas in the head, but also a disposition of the heart."† Now if saving faith is an exercise of the heart, loving God, as well as of the intellect, weighing evidence, it is certainly a fruit of regeneration; for "every one that loveth is born of God." Let this argument be carefully weighed. Either the true believer loves God, or he does not. If he does not, his faith does not differ essentially from that of devils. If he does, he is regenerated; for so declares the Apostle John in the passage just quoted. Moreover, "love is the fulfilling of the law" of God, and therefore love is holiness. Consequently every one who loves God, has something of holiness, which, it is admitted, none have before regeneration.

The doctrine of the Methodist Church is, that the sinner first exercises true faith, and afterward is regenerated; but the Scriptures do plainly teach the converse; that is, that the sinner is regenerated, and, as an effect

* Rom. 10 : 10. † Sermon on Salvation by Faith.

of regeneration, immediately exercises faith; just as when our Saviour raised Lazarus from the dead, he was first made alive, and then began to breathe and perform other living acts. "Whosoever believeth that Jesus is the Christ, is born of God."* It is not said that he who believes *shall be* regenerated, quickened, or born again. Regeneration is never promised on condition of believing, but the exercise of faith is declared to be conclusive evidence that regeneration has already taken place; just as the fact that a man who has been hurt, breathes, is clear evidence that he is alive.

If, then, it is true, as it certainly is, that before regeneration there is nothing morally good in men,—that they do not exercise true repentance or saving faith; it follows inevitably, that when God regenerates the heart of a sinner, he does not perform this work on account of any moral goodness in him, or because he is better than others. Of his own mercy and for reasons not made known to us, he performs the work. He did not purpose to do this work because he foresaw that the sinner would repent and believe the gospel, for until he is regenerated he exercises neither repentance nor faith.

It is, then, clear, first, that God is the author of regeneration; secondly, that he regenerates the hearts of men not accidentally, but designedly; and, thirdly, that the purpose to regenerate any sinner was not formed on the ground of repentance and faith foreseen, but of the sovereign mercy of God, and for reasons not revealed to us.

IV. *The purposes of God to regenerate any of the human race are* ETERNAL. All his purposes, as we have

---

* 1 John 5: 1.

proved in the first part of this work, are eternal. Let us again place the point distinctly before our minds. God regenerates the heart of a sinner to-day, and he does this work in fulfilment of a gracious *purpose.* This is a wise purpose, founded upon the best reasons, though they may be unknown to us. *When* was this purpose formed? Has God learned anything concerning this man which he did not always know? Certainly not, for then he would not be omniscient. But since all intelligent purposes are formed in view of *reasons,* and since all the reasons in view of which this purpose was formed were *from eternity* before the Divine Mind, the purpose itself must be eternal. As already proved, every new purpose formed, and every change of purpose, proclaims the being forming or changing it *imperfect.*

Nor can any one reasonably object to the eternity of the Divine purposes. If the work done is a good work (and certainly Christians and angels rejoice in it as such), there can be no possible objection to the doctrine that God always designed doing it. The purpose to do a good work is a good purpose, for which God is to be praised. Every objection against the *eternity* of the Divine purpose to renew a sinner's heart, lies with equal force against the formation of such purpose at all. If the decree of Election destroys the free agency of the person chosen to life, the result would be the same if the purpose exist one month, one day, one hour, one moment before the work is done. If there be anything unjust in it, the injustice is in the purpose itself, not in the period of its formation. It is wrong for a man to determine to do an unjust thing, but it matters not whether such determination be formed years or moments before it is executed. The length of time changes not the moral character of the purpose.

In these four propositions the doctrine of Election is fully embraced. God is the author of regeneration. In every case he performs the work *designedly*, not *accidentally*. His purpose to regenerate the heart of any sinner is not founded upon anything good foreseen in him,—on any foresight of faith or repentance. God formed the purpose before the world began. The sum of the four propositions is, that God from eternity purposed to renew, sanctify, and save a certain portion of the human race for the glory of his sovereign grace. Which of these propositions can be successfully assailed? Will it be denied that God is the author of regeneration? But this truth is admitted by the more evangelical Arminians, such as Wesley and Watson; and to deny it, is to run into fundamental error. Will it be said that God does this work *accidentally*, not *designedly?* None will take a position so absurd! Will it be asserted that God regenerates only those in whom he sees something morally good, as repentance and faith? Then you have moral goodness or holiness before regeneration,—life before quickening,—or living acts before life. This is too absurd to be maintained for a moment. Will it be denied that the purpose to regenerate is *eternal?* But is not Election *in time* just as objectionable as Election in *eternity?* Beside, if God forms new purposes, he must gain new knowledge, and is, consequently, an imperfect, mutable Being! There is no way of escape from the doctrine without running into the most serious, if not fundamental error. This assertion will be more fully proved in the next chapter.

CHAPTER IV.

THE SCRIPTURAL ARGUMENT CONTINUED AND THE PRACTICAL IMPORTANCE OF THE DOCTRINE SHOWN.

No Christian, we believe, objects to the doctrine of Election, provided he understands it. All the truly pious rejoice to acknowledge God as the author of the great change which has passed upon them; and all acknowledge that they were not renewed in heart because of any good existing in them, or done by them. With the grateful Psalmist, they all say,—"Not unto us, O Lord, not unto us, but unto thy name give glory, for thy mercy and for thy truth's sake."* And with Paul,—"By the grace of God I am what I am."†. And surely no one would be less grateful, if assured that God always designed to renew his heart and lead him to Christ.

But the doctrine of *Reprobation*, as it is called, presents difficulties to the minds of many. What is this doctrine? The Confession of Faith teaches that "The rest of mankind [not elected] God was pleased, according to the unsearchable counsel of his own will, whereby he extendeth or withholdeth mercy as he pleaseth, for the glory of his sovereign power over his creatures, to pass by and to ordain them to dishonor and wrath for their sin, to the praise of his glorious justice." Now

* Ps. 115: 1.

† 1 Cor. 5: 10.

Arminians agree with us, that on the day of judgment God will pronounce sentence of eternal condemnation upon multitudes of men. "Then shall he say unto them on the left hand, Depart from me, ye cursed, into everlasting fire, prepared for the devil and his angels. And these shall go away into everlasting punishment." Will this fearful sentence be just? Arminians agree with us tnat it will, because it will be a sentence of merited punishment *for their sin*. Then can there be any objection to saying, that God purposed from eternity to pronounce this just sentence? He foresaw the sin of the finally impenitent, and for their sin he purposed to inflict upon them the just penalty of his law. Can any one object to this? Can it be unjust in God to purpose to do a just act?

But it will be objected, that according to our doctrine, God *passed by* the non-elect, and did not give them the grace necessary to lead them to repentance, and then condemns them for not doing what they could not possibly do. To this objection we have two answers to make, viz:

1. Every man is, from the very nature of his mind, a free moral agent, and therefore justly held accountable for all his actions. Every one is bound to obey God, and if he refuse, is justly exposed to the penalty of the moral law.

2. Even Arminians are obliged to acknowledge that God does make great differences in the treatment of the human family, not only in the distribution of temporal blessings, but of spiritual gifts also,—a difference which compels them, if they would be consistent, to hold the doctrine of Election. As we have already seen, they

hold to the doctrine of a particular providence, and to a divine election of individuals and nations to peculiar religious privileges. The Rev. Richard Watson says of God's providential dispensations:—"These dispensations are not only instruments of prevention, but designed means of salvation, preparatory to, and co-operative with, those agencies by which that result can only be directly produced." The same writer says:—"Another benefit, granted for the same end, is the revelation of the will of God and the declaration of his purposes of grace as to man's actual redemption. These purposes have been declared to man, with great inequality we grant, a mystery which we are not able to explain; but we have the testimony of God in his own word, though we cannot in many cases trace the process of the revelation, that in no case, that in no nation 'has he left himself without witness.'"* Now observe, it is a fact admitted by Mr. Watson, a fact indeed which none can deny, that God in his providence bestows upon some individuals and upon some nations the abundant means of salvation, which are withheld from others. In our country, for example, all have access to the written word of God, and the great majority may hear the voice of the ordained ministers of Christ expounding his word and calling them to repentance, and may attend upon the ordinances of his house. In pagan lands, multitudes, just as depraved as we, and therefore needing all the advantages we enjoy to bring them to repentance, have no knowledge whatever of God's written word,—do not

* Theol. Inst., pt. 2, ch. 23.

even know that such a book as the Bible exists,—never hear the voice of the living ministry; but have been born and reared under the influence of a dark, degrading and cruel superstition. Now, will any one pretend that those benighted pagans have opportunities of being saved equal to ours? They are as deeply depraved as the people of Christian countries. Are the same or equally powerful influences brought to bear upon them to lead them to God, and engage them in his service? Let us admit, though it cannot be proved, that the Holy Spirit exerts upon the minds of such persons the same degree of influence which is exerted upon those who enjoy abundantly the means of grace; yet is that degree of influence, in the absence of the written word and the ordinances of the gospel, at all equal to that exerted by these means upon persons in Christian lands? Certainly not. Now the influence exerted in connection with the appointed means of grace, does result in the conversion and salvation of many. Is it not fair, then, to conclude that if the same means were employed in pagan lands, a much larger number would be saved, than without them? If not, we are forced to the conclusion, that the preaching of the gospel is of no importance, except in the moralizing and happy influence it exerts in the present life. But if there is abundant evidence that the heathen would in great numbers turn to God, if they were brought under the same influences we in Christian lands enjoy, then does it not follow that God, in his all-wise providence having not sent them the gospel, has really *passed by* them and left them to perish? If the sending of the gospel to a people, with the divine influence accompanying it, does not amount to a *personal election*, most assuredly the withholding of it from a people amounts generally to *reprobation*.

We readily admit, with Mr. Wesley, that "inasmuch as to them [the heathen] little is given, of them little will be required,"—that "no more will be expected of them, than the living up to the light they had."* But they are totally depraved as others, and love to sin as much as others. And as a matter of fact, they are generally extremely degraded. For example, Mr. Wesley describes the inhabitants of the South Sea Islands as "heathens of the basest sort, many of them inferior to the beasts of the field," as "more savage than lions," and exclaims:—"See the real dignity of human nature! Here it appears in its genuine purity, not polluted either by those 'general corrupters, kings,' or by the least tincture of religion!" The Mohammedans he describes as "in general as utter strangers to all true religion as their four-footed brethren; as void of mercy as lions and tigers; as much given up to brutal lusts as bulls and goats; so that they are in truth a disgrace to human nature, and a plague to all that are under the iron yoke."† Now does not the leaving of the heathen and the Mohammedans in this degraded state, destitute of the light of the gospel, amount in effect to passing by them and leaving them to perish in their sins? Such certainly is the truth, at least in a multitude of instances. God has left them in this state, and he of course purposed to do what he has done.

* Sermon on Faith.

† Sermon on the Genera Spread of the Gospel.

But the difference which God makes as to the means of grace and salvation, are not confined to nations or bodies of people. In Christian countries, where all enjoy the means of grace to some extent, those means are enjoyed by families and individuals in very different degrees. Some enjoy the inestimable blessing of being born of pious parents, of being taught the glorious doctrines and principles of Christianity from infancy, and of bowing from day to day around the family altar. And from early childhood they are guarded against corrupting sentiments and influences, receive the instructions of the Sabbath-school, and sit under an able, evangelical and faithful ministry. Others are born of degraded and vicious parents, from early childhood imbibe false principles, and form their character under demoralizing influences, discouraged if not prevented from enjoying the means of grace at all. Between these extremes the means of salvation are enjoyed in various degrees by different families and individuals. And these privileges, let it not be forgotten, like those which exist in different nations, depend in no degree upon the moral character or conduct of the individuals whose eternal destiny is so intimately connected with them. As one man is born in the midst of the degrading idolatry of India without any particular fault of his, so is another born in the United States of America without any merit entitling him to so great a privilege. And so one is born of Infidel parents and in the midst of vice, and another under pure Christian influence, without any difference as to ill desert or merit. It cannot be denied, then, that the means of grace are enjoyed in vastly different degrees by different individuals; that God has chosen to make this difference in his providence, without any foresight of goodness in the favored class, or of peculiar demerit in the other.

Now, that the force of the argument may be distinctly seen, let us select two individuals from the two classes. One, we will suppose, is the son of eminently wise and godly parents, by whom he is from infancy trained up in the nurture and admonition of the Lord, and who afford to him every opportunity of being taught the truth as it is in Jesus, and are careful to bring him under the power of the gospel in every practical way, while he is the subject of their constant and fervent prayers. The other is born of parents who reject, ridicule and despise Christianity, and who are careful to prevent his being brought under the power of the gospel. His character is formed under the influence of corrupt sentiments, and of evil and corrupting example. The tendency of all his associations is to withdraw him entirely from Christianity. The former becomes a devoted Christian, and spends his days in the service of his Redeemer. The latter embraces the corrupt sentiments inculcated in childhood, follows the evil example set him, lives in wickedness and dies impenitent. The one is saved, the other lost. Now will any one deny that there is a vast difference in the influences favorable to salvation brought to bear on these two persons ? Will any one deny that the opportunities of being saved enjoyed by the former, are far greater than those enjoyed by the latter ? Will it not be admitted by every candid individual, that if the two had changed places, they would probably have changed characters also ?—that if the son of the godly parents had been the son of infidels, and had lived under the same corrupting influences, he would, in all probability, have died in his sins? But God in his mysterious providence placed them under widely different influences, and the results are widely different. And did he not foresee these different results even before either was born? Most assuredly. Then does not the difference providentially made, amount to an election of the one to life and salvation, and a passing by the other, leaving him in his sins?

Take another case of frequent occurrence. A thoughtless individual is induced to go to the house of God, which he is not accustomed to attend. The subject of discourse is precisely adapted to his character. He is deeply impressed, and becomes a disciple of Christ. Those who believe in a special providence, will admit that God sent the sinner to hear this discourse. There are others in the same state of mind, who, had they heard the same discourse, might have been similarly affected; just as the Saviour said concerning Sodom, that if the mighty works done in Capernaum had been done in that city, it would not have been destroyed. A difference is made providentially, upon which turns the salvation of souls. It amounts to an election of the one, and a passing by of the others.

There is a time in the life of every one who becomes a Christian, when a deeper impression than ever before is made on his mind, which results in his determination to receive Jesus Christ as his Saviour. This deeper impression is made either by an extraordinary influence of the Holy Spirit, or by peculiar circumstances or occurrences, or by both combined. If the impression be caused by an extraordinary influence of the Spirit, which is not exerted in an equal degree on others, it amounts to an election or an "effectual calling," in the one case, and a *passing by* in the others. If it be caused by peculiar providential circumstances or occurrences which do not attend others, the result is the same,—it amounts to an election. If it be caused by the combined influence of the Spirit and of peculiar circumstances, it is still the same. For in either case an influence is exerted which effects the conversion of the one individual, and which, had it been exerted equally, might have effected the conversion of others. For example, Saul of Tarsus was arrested on his way to Damascus by a light brighter than the sun, and by the voice of the Son of God; and he was converted. Now if the doctrine be true, that the sinner exercises repentance and faith before he is regenerated, we may say with certainty that there have been multitudes who have died in sin, who, if they had been arrested in the same manner, would have been converted. But God chose thus to arrest Saul, for the glory of his grace, and to pass by others,—knowing what the results would be. If, then, he chose to make so great a difference in his treatment of individuals, knowing the result, did he not choose Saul of Tarsus to salvation, and pass by others?

In a word, our Arminian friends must deny the doctrine of a particular providence, and deny that the enjoyment of the means of grace has any influence in securing the salvation of men; or they must cease to oppose the doctrine of Election.

What now is the precise difference between the Methodists and the Presbyterians on this subject? Is it, that according to Methodists, God in his providential dispensations treats all alike, while, according to Presbyterians and other Calvinists, he makes a difference by giving to some blessings which he gives not to others? No; the Methodists acknowledge that he makes great differences; and here they agree with us. Do the Methodists hold that the means of salvation are granted equally to all, while Calvinists hold that in this respect God makes great differences? No; the Methodists acknowledge that he has chosen both nations and individuals to peculiar religious privileges, which he has not conferred on others; and here again they agree with us. Do the Methodists hold that these differences depend upon the *moral character* of nations or of individuals, while Calvinists hold that God, in the bestowment of religious privileges, acts as a sovereign? No; they do not pretend that one child was born of pious parents because of its merit, and another of infidel parents as a punishment of its demerit. They admit that the election of bodies of people and of individuals to peculiar religious privileges, is sovereign and unconditional. "God has a right," says Mr. Watson, "to elect whom he pleases to enjoy special privileges; in this there is no unrighteousness."* Both Arminians and Calvinists hold, that as to the means of salvation, God makes a great difference in the treatment of nations and of individuals; but Calvinists believe that God exerts on the minds of some a more powerful influence of his Spirit than upon others, thus inducing the former to choose the way of life to the glory of his sovereign grace. In other words, both Calvinists and Arminians agree that

* Theol. Inst., pt. 2, ch. 26.

God makes great differences in the influences he brings to bear upon the minds of different individuals to effect their conversion; but Calvinists believe the difference to be *somewhat greater* than Arminians are disposed to allow. Indeed, if Mr. Wesley is a fair representative of Arminian Methodism, the difference is even less than I have stated. For after speaking of God's *assisting* sinners to make a happy choice, he says: "Not that I deny that there are exempt cases, wherein

'The overwhelming power of saving grace'

does for a time work as irresistibly as lightning falling from heaven. But I speak of God's general manner of working,"* etc. Now, no Calvinist would or could use stronger language than this, concerning "effectual calling." If it be true that God exerts upon some persons a converting influence irresistible as lightning, most certainly they are regenerated. And if he purposed to exert such an influence, he purposed to regenerate them; and this is, to all intents and purposes, the doctrine of Election. For if such an influence may be exerted in one case, why not in another?

The truth is, Methodists and other Arminians of the more evangelical class, hold too much evangelical truth to oppose with any consistency the doctrine of Election. Those who deny the doctrines of Divine providence, imputation, original sin, and regeneration, stand in a much better position to assail it. It has always been associated with the fundamental doctrines of Christianity, and the opposers of these doctrines have ever been among its most zealous and consistent assailants.

* Sermon on the General Spread of the Gospel.

CHAPTER V.

THE SCRIPTURAL ARGUMENT CONTINUED.

Having answered the most plausible objections to the doctrine of Election, and having presented some conclusive evidence that it is clearly taught in the Scriptures, we proceed to the consideration of a number of passages of Scripture not yet noticed, which seem to us to establish it beyond reasonable doubt. We design to present and examine the interpretations given of those passages by eminent Arminian writers, and we invite the reader's particular attention to the inquiry, whether Arminians or Calvinists give the more plain and obvious interpretation. This is a matter of great importance; for it cannot be doubted, that the apparent and obvious meaning of the language of the inspired writers, is generally its true meaning; and those doctrines are much to be suspected which can be sustained only by far-fetched and ingenious interpretations.

I. Let us first examine the passages in which those who become believers are represented as *given* to Christ. "All that the Father giveth me, shall come to me; and him that cometh to me, I will in no wise cast out."* Two things are clear from this passage, viz: first, that some persons are given by the Father to the Son; and,

---

* John 6: 37.

second, that all such persons will certainly come to him, or will believe in him. Dr. Adam Clark explains the passage thus: "Those who come at the call of God, he is represented here as *giving to Christ,* because it is through his blood alone, that they can be saved. * * Our Lord may here also refer to the *calling* of the *Gentiles;* for these, according to the ancient promise (Ps. ii.), were given to Christ; and they, on the preaching of the gospel, gladly came unto him." Now as to the first part of this exposition, it is palpably incorrect. For the Saviour says, all that the Father *giveth,* shall *come;* but Dr. Clarke makes him say, all that *come* to Christ the Father *gives* to him. In our Saviour's language, the *giving* is first and the *coming* is consequent upon it; but in Dr. Clarke's interpretation, the *coming* is first and the *giving* is consequent upon it. He makes the Saviour say precisely the reverse of what he intended to say. But if our Lord refers to the calling of the *Gentiles,* as the Doctor supposed, then *all* the Gentiles must come to him; but the Gentiles have not all come to him. Nor indeed is there the slightest evidence of any such reference.

Dr. Whitby expounds the passage thus:—"To be given of the Father is to be convinced by the miracles which God had wrought by him to testify the truth of his mission, and thereby to set his seal unto him, that he was the Messiah, the Son of God; and to be willing upon these testimonies to own him as such, laying aside all those unreasonable prejudices and carnal affections which obstructed their coming to him." This is truly a remarkable exposition. To be *given,* says Dr. Whitby, is to be *convinced,* and to be *willing* to act accordingly!

How did he discover that the word *give* is synonymous with the words *convince* and *willing?* Surely we need not spend time in refuting such an interpretation.

The Rev. Richard Watson, not satisfied with these interpretations of his Arminian brethren, adopts an entirely different one. He says, the phrase, to be "*given*" by the Father to Christ, had a special application to those pious Jews who waited for redemption at Jerusalem: those who read and *believed* the writings of Moses, and who were thus prepared, by more spiritual views than the rest, though they were not unmixed with obscurity, to receive Christ as the Messiah. * * * Taught of the Father, led into the sincere belief and general spiritual understanding of the Scriptures as to the Messiah, when Christ appeared they were 'drawn' and 'given' to him as the now visible and accredited Head, Teacher, Lord and Saviour of the Church."* There are two insuperable objections to this interpretation, viz: 1. Without the least evidence to support it, it gives to phraseology which is *general* in its obvious meaning, a *particular* and *very limited* application. Even Mr. Watson would not deny that multitudes, beside the few Jews who were then enlightened, were given to Christ. This the Saviour teaches, when he, in that remarkable prayer in the seventeenth chapter of the gospel by John, says:—"As thou hast given him power over all flesh, that he should give eternal life to as many as thou hast given him." Why, then, when the Saviour speaks of *all* that the Father giveth him, should his meaning be restricted to a few individuals? 2. But this interpretation is

* Theol. Inst., pt. 2, ch. 27.

inconsistent with the context. In the thirty-ninth verse he says:—"And this is the Father's will which hath sent me, that of all which he hath given me I should lose nothing, but should raise it up again at the last day." This language, as Dr. Clarke admits, has reference to all believers in all ages. He gives the sense of it thus:—"It is the will of God, that every soul who believes should continue in the faith, and have a resurrection unto life eternal." Why should the phrase "all that the Father giveth," be confined in its meaning to a few individuals in the thirty-seventh verse, and the same phrase in the thirty-ninth verse be understood to refer to all who believe in all ages?

Evidently the three different interpretations of this passage, given by these three eminent Arminian writers, are forced and inconsistent. What is its obvious meaning? Certainly it means, that the Father has given *some* of the human race to the Son, and that all such will believe in him. God sent his Son into the world to become "a man of sorrows and acquainted with grief,"—to die a most painful and ignominious death. These sufferings were not to be in vain. The promise of the Father was that "he shall see of the travail of his soul, and be satisfied." By the quickening power of the Holy Spirit, those given to him should be willing to receive him. He would effectually call them, and they would willingly come. This passage, then, and the other passages containing similar phraseology, evidently teach the doctrine of Election.

II. There is another class of Scripture passages, which teach that those who become believers in Christ, *were chosen or elected before the foundation of the world.*—

"Blessed be the God and Father of our Lord Jesus Christ, who hath blessed us with all spiritual blessings in heavenly places in Christ: according as he hath chosen us in him, before the foundation of the world, that we should be holy and without blame before him in love: having predestinated us unto the adoption of children by Jesus Christ unto himself, according to the good pleasure of his will, to the praise of the glory of his grace, wherein he hath made us accepted in the beloved."* The apostle praises God, because of the abundant spiritual blessings he had bestowed upon himself and the Ephesian Christians. These blessings had been bestowed in accordance with a Divine purpose formed before the foundation of the world, viz: that they should be sanctified, and that they should enjoy the adoption of children. God purposed to sanctify them and to adopt them as his children, and *therefore* he bestowed upon them "all spiritual blessings in heavenly places in Christ." These things God purposed to do, not because of foreseen faith and works, but "according to the good pleasure of his will, to the praise of the glory of his grace." Such appears to be the obvious meaning of the language of the apostle.

Mr. Watson admits that the apostle in this passage speaks of Election "as the *means* of faith, and of faith as the *end* of election;" but he contends that he does not speak of *personal election*, but of "the collective election of the whole body of Christians." The apostle, he says, speaks "of the election of believing Jews and Gentiles into the Church of God; in other words,

---

* Eph. 1: 3–5.

of the eternal purpose of God, upon the publication of the gospel, to constitute his visible Church no longer upon the ground of natural descent from Abraham, but upon the foundation of faith in Christ."* Mr. Watson agrees with Calvinists on the following points, viz: 1. That the purpose of God here mentioned, is properly *eternal.* 2. That the election is not founded upon foreseen faith, but is *in order to* faith, and faith is its *end.* But he will have it an election of believing Jews and Gentiles, to constitute the Church of Christ. To this interpretation there are insuperable objections. The apostle says not a word about the constituting of this visible Church, and not a word about choosing either Jews or Gentiles to be in the Church. He speaks, first, of an election *unto holiness,*—"that we should be holy and without blame before him in love." Now holiness is a thing strictly *personal,* and so is love; and therefore an election to holiness and to love, can be nothing else than a *personal election.* Again, this is an election "unto the adoption of *children.*" But believers as individuals, and such only, are adopted as God's children; and therefore the election unto the adoption of children must be a *personal election.* Moreover, the apostle uses the personal pronoun *us,* showing that he meant to speak only of *persons,* not of Jews and Gentiles generally. Beside, Mr. Watson's exposition of the passage is contradictory. He admits that the election here spoken of is an election *unto faith,*—an election "as a *means* of faith;" and yet he contends that it is an election "of

*Theol. Inst., pt. 2, ch. 26.

believing Jews and Gentiles into the Church of God." If it is an election in order to faith, how can it be an election of *believers?* The Calvinistic interpretation of this portion of Scripture is evidently in accordance with the obvious meaning of the language of Inspiration. Before the foundation of the world God purposed to renew and sanctify these Ephesian Christians, that they might be "holy and without blame before him in love," and to grant unto them the adoption of children. This purpose was not founded upon faith and obedience foreseen, for they were chosen *in order that* they might be holy; and faith is one of the exercises of holiness. God predestinated them according to the good pleasure of his will, and to the praise of the glory of his grace. And at the proper time, in fulfillment of this gracious purpose, he quickened them and blessed them with all spiritual blessings.

This doctrine is distinctly taught by the same Apostle in the Second Epistle to the Thessalonians, where, speaking of the great apostasy, he says:—"But we are bound to give thanks always to God for you, brethren beloved of the Lord, because God hath from the beginning chosen you to salvation, through sanctification of the Spirit, and belief of the truth: whereunto he called you by our gospel, to the obtaining of the glory of our Lord Jesus Christ."* We have here *the end* to which they were chosen, viz: *salvation; the means* by which this end was to be effected, viz: sanctification of the Spirit, and belief of the truth; *the period* when they were

---

* Ch. 2 13, 14.

chosen, viz: from the beginning, or from eternity; and the fulfillment of the purpose in their effectual calling to the obtaining of the glory of Christ.

Mr. Watson strangely affirms, that "the calling of the members of this Church is not represented by the apostle as the *effect* of their having been chosen, but on the contrary, their election is spoken of as the effect of 'the sanctification of the Spirit and belief of the truth.'" But look carefully at the apostle's language. He says God had chosen them *to salvation.* Did he choose them because they had been sanctified by the Spirit, and had believed the truth? No; for, in the first place, the sanctification of the Spirit is an important part of the salvation to which they were chosen. Salvation or deliverance from sin is effected by the work of the Spirit on the heart. And, secondly, the phrase "*through* sanctification of the Spirit," does not mean *on account of* the sanctification of the Spirit. Salvation is the thing, *the end,* to which they were chosen; and this end was to be accomplished through or *by means of* sanctification of the Spirit and belief of the truth.

Dr. Clarke does not hold, as does Mr. Watson, that these Christians were chosen because they were sanctified; but he refers the whole passage to the purpose of God to call the Gentiles to the privileges of the gospel. He paraphrases the apostle's language thus:—"In your *calling,* God has shown the *purpose* that he had formed from the *beginning,* to call the Gentiles to the same privileges with the Jews," etc. But, unfortunately for this exposition, the apostle says not a word in the whole of the connection, concerning Jews and Gentiles. He predicts the great Roman apostasy, which was to occur in the Church, and while he speaks of the "strong delusion" which would be sent upon many, he gives thanks that God had from the beginning chosen the Thessalonian Christians to a better end, even to salvation, and had appointed the means necessary to that end.

Very similar to this passage, is the language of Peter, addressed to the strangers scattered throughout Pontus, etc.:—"Elect according to the foreknowledge of God the Father, through sanctification of the Spirit, unto obedience and sprinkling of the blood of Jesus Christ." They were elected, not because God foresaw that they would obey, nor because they had obeyed, but *unto* obedience, in order that they might obey. They were elected unto obedience, just as they were elected unto the sprinkling of the blood of Christ, that is, to the enjoyment of the blessings of the atonement. The election of God is first, the efficacious calling consequent upon the election, and obedience the effect of this calling.

We are thus conducted to another class of Scriptures which speak of what the Westminster Confession terms "*effectual calling*." Paul, writing to the Corinthians, uses the following language :—"For the Jews require a sign, and the Greeks seek after wisdom. But we preach Christ crucified, unto the Jews a stumbling-block, and unto the Greeks foolishness; but unto them which are called, both Jews and Greeks, Christ the power of God, and the wisdom of God.' * Observe, the call of the gospel was given indiscriminately to Jews and Greeks; the apostles delivered to all the same message, and extended to all the same invitation. Of this call the

* 1 Cor. 1: 22–24.

Saviour speaks, when he says:—"Many are called, but few chosen." Both Jews and Greeks rejected the gospel message, though on very different grounds. The former desired to see a sign from heaven, before they would believe; and the latter were displeased with the simplicity of the gospel,—seeing in it nothing of the intricate and obscure speculations of the Grecian philosophy, which they mistook for wisdom. The depravity of the human heart leads all men, when left to themselves, to reject the gospel; though they justify themselves by very different excuses.

But although the general disposition of both Jews and Greeks was to reject the gospel, yet to some, both Jews and Greeks, it was the power of God and the wisdom of God. They saw in it a wisdom far above the wisdom of men, and felt in its doctrines a power to purify and elevate, which only God can exert. These the apostle describes as "*them which are called*." They evidently had a peculiar call, an *effectual* call; for it resulted in their conversion to Christ. What was this call? It was not the preaching of the gospel, for others, equally with them, had this call. It was evidently, then, that influence of the Holy Spirit by which they were changed in heart, and made willing to receive Christ as their Saviour. Of this *calling* Peter speaks, when he teaches Christians to show forth "the praises of him who hath called them out of darkness into his marvelous light."* Of this *calling* Paul writes in the Epistle to the Romans:—"For whom he did foreknow, he also did predestinate to be conformed to the image

* 1 Pet. 2: 9.

of his Son, that he might be the first-born among many brethren. Moreover, whom he did predestinate, them he also called: and whom he called, them he also justified: and whom he justified, them he also glorified."* The apostle is here proving, that "all things work together for good to them that love God, to them who are the called according to his purpose;" and he proves it by showing that God originally purposed to save them, and that he is now, in his providence and by his grace, carrying out this purpose. Let us note the several steps presented in the text. The persons spoken of were *foreknown.* Were they foreknown as *believers?* Did God foresee that they would believe and receive the gospel, and was his predestination of them founded upon such foreknowledge? Mr. Watson answers these questions affirmatively; we, for several clear reasons, answer them in the negative. First, they were first foreknown and predestinated, and were called because thus foreknown; but according to Arminianism, all receive the same call, and of course that call is not based on a foreknowledge of faith. Secondly, the apostle says, "whom he called, them [the same individuals] he justified, and whom he justified, them he also glorified;" but according to Arminianism, many who receive this call reject it, and consequently are not justified, much less glorified. The apostle teaches, that all who receive this call, are justified and glorified; but Arminianism teaches, that much the larger portion are never justified at all. Thirdly, they are predestinated *to be conformed* to the image of God, not predestinated because

* Rom. 8: 29, 30.

God foresaw that they would be conformed. And, fourthly, no one, as we have already proved, ever exercises true faith, until he is regenerated. Consequently, God could foreknow them as believers, only because he purposed to renew their hearts and dispose them to receive Christ. It is worthy of remark, that Dr. Clarke, who was not a less zealous Arminian than Mr. Watson, differs materially from him in explaining the word *foreknow.* He says: — "To *foreknow,* here signifies to *design before,* or at the first forming of the scheme: to bestow the *favor* and *privilege* of being God's people upon any set of men (as Rom. xi, 2). This is the *foundation,* or first step of our salvation; namely, the *purpose* and *grace of God,* which was given us in Christ Jesus before the world began (2 Tim. i, 9). Then, he *knew* or *favored* us, for in this sense the word *to know* is taken in a great variety of places, both in the Old and New Testaments. * * * When God knew us at the forming of the gospel scheme, or when he intended to bestow on us the privilege of being his people, he then *destinated* or designed us to be conformed to the image of his Son: and as he *destinated* or *determined* us then to this very high honor and happiness, he *predestinated, foreordained,* or *predetermined* us to it." We are willing to take this general exposition of the words *foreknow* and *predestinate.* God, first, *foreknew* or designed to *favor* the persons. Then, secondly, he predestinated them *to holiness,* or predetermined to sanctify them; for God is the author of sanctification. Then, thirdly, he, in accordance with his foreknowledge and purpose, *called* them. And it is clear that this call was effectual, because the same persons who received the call were justified, as they could not be unless they believed. And, fourth, the same persons were *glorified*. Thus the apostle gives the general manner of the Divine procedure in the salvation of men. They are chosen, called, justified, glorified. And because God is now carrying out his eternal purpose to save them, we know, as the apostle argues, that all things work together for their good. Having determined *the end*, God is employing the best means and agencies for its accomplishment. Those means and agencies are his Word, his Ordinances, his Providences, and his Spirit.

Many other passages of Scripture might be adduced in confirmation of the doctrine of Election, but the evidence already furnished is amply sufficient to satisfy the unprejudiced mind. There is no part of Scripture, however plain the language, upon which an ingenious writer may not put a plausible interpretation contrary to its obvious import; but we ask the candid reader to determine for himself, in the fear of God, whether the interpretations we have given of the passages quoted is not more in accordance with the obvious import of the language of Inspiration, than the different and contradictory interpretations of Arminians, who, while they agree in asserting that those passages do not teach Election, cannot agree what they do teach. Do not these efforts to fix upon those passages a sense consistent with Arminianism, look more like a defense of their Creed against the Bible, than an impartial exposition of its language?

CHAPTER VI.

PRACTICAL BEARINGS OF THE WHOLE DOCTRINE OF DIVINE FOREORDINATION.

The doctrine of Divine foreordination is not a mere metaphysical dogma without practical bearing. It has ever been associated with the great doctrines of the Cross, and its practical effects have been decided and happy.

1. It gives exalted and just views of the character of God. It presents him as, in his infinite wisdom, fixing upon the noblest *ends* and adopting the best *means* for their accomplishment. He purposed to glorify his name in the highest degree by the redemption of an innumerable multitude of men. For this purpose he created the world and formed man. His all-wise plans were not frustrated by the temptation and fall of man, nor will they fail through the wickedness of men. The fall he chose, for wise reasons, to permit; and surely the wrath of man shall praise him: the remainder of wrath he will restrain (Psalm lxxvi. 10). "The Lord reigneth; let the earth rejoice; let the multitude of Isles be glad thereof;" "The Lord reigneth; let the people tremble." "He doeth according to his will in the army of heaven, and among the inhabitants of the earth: and none can stay his hand, or say unto him, what doest thou?" "For the Lord of hosts hath purposed, and

who shall disannul it? and his hand is stretched out, and who shall turn it back?" His purposes originated in eternity, and are carried forward without change to eternity. They extend to all his works, and control all events. He "worketh all things after the counsel of his will." All are made to contribute in one way or another to the great end, and yet in no single instance is the free agency of his rational creatures impaired. God is sovereign, and man is free. "Great is the Lord, and greatly to be praised; and his greatness is unsearchable."

2. This doctrine gives the greatest encouragement to virtue. It teaches, that the path of duty is in all cases the path of safety and of happiness. Not only has God established a general connection between sin and misery, and between holiness and happiness; but his providence and grace combine to make the path of true virtue the way to real prosperity and lasting blessedness. The providence of God is over all his works,—especially over his people: and in his providence God is simply executing his eternal purposes. He is conducting his people along the path his infinite wisdom has chosen for them, and therefore "all things work together for good to them that love God, to them who are the called according to his purpose." He can restrain, direct and overrule the actions of wicked men without interfering with their free agency. The believer may, therefore, adopt the language of the Psalmist, and say:—"What time I am afraid, I will trust in thee. In God I will praise his word, in God I have put my trust; I will not fear what flesh can do unto me."* But if, as Arminianism teaches, God cannot control the passions and direct the

* Ps. 56: 3, 4.

conduct of men without destroying their free agency, where is there safety for the righteous? Indeed, how can there be a particular providence, if the doctrine of Divine foreordination is not true? If there be a *wise* providence over men, it must be directed to some worthy end or ends,—it must be the carrying out of plans or purposes,—the execution of wise designs. But Arminians object, that, such purposes destroy man's free agency and make God the author of sin. Then there can be no particular providence, at least so far as the passions and actions of men are concerned in passing events. Where, then, we again ask, is the ground of safety to the righteous?

3. The tendency of this doctrine is to fill the hearts of Christians with humility and with gratitude. By nature all men, according to this doctrine, are totally depraved and under just condemnation. By practice they are rebels, justly exposed to the wrath of God. God was under no obligation to offer them salvation. The mission of Christ, therefore, was purely gracious, and his work of obedience and suffering a purely gracious work. "God so LOVED the world that he gave his only begotten Son." The atonement of Christ is to be regarded as an amazing exhibition of love and of grace toward those who deserve to perish.

"O for this love let rocks and hills
Their lasting silence break,
And all harmonious human tongues
The Saviour's praises speak."

But Arminianism teaches, that it would have been unjust that Adam's posterity should have perished without the offer of salvation. God was, therefore, it would seem, under some obligation to provide a Saviour or a method of deliverance. The mission and the work of Christ consequently cannot be regarded as purely gracious. It is, at least in part, a matter of *justice* to the unfortunate race of man. Now it is impossible that this view of the subject should beget either humility or gratitude. If men view their original sin as merely their *misfortune,* they will scarcely consider it a cause of deep humility of soul; and so far as they regard the work of Christ as a work of *justice* to them, they will not be likely to feel very grateful for it. The gratitude of Christians toward their Redeemer will be proportioned to their views of their ill desert. So our Saviour teaches in the parable of the two debtors (Luke vii. 40),—by which he accounted for the extraordinary love of the woman, who was a sinner, and who washed his feet with her tears and wiped them with the hairs of her head:—"Wherefore, I say unto thee, her sins, which are many, are forgiven; for she loved much: but to whom little is forgiven, the same loveth little."

Again, according to the doctrine of Divine foreordination, God is the author of all that is pure in the Christian's heart. He saw him "dead in trespasses and sins." He purposed to renew his heart, not because of anything in the sinner moving him thereto, nor because of any foreseen co-operation on his part, but simply of his sovereign mercy. So that the most devoted Christian, comparing his present condition and character with his former condition and character, must say emphatically with Paul:—"By the grace of God I am what I am." And of all his good works he must say:—"I labored; yet not I, but the grace of God which was with me."

But Arminianism rejects the doctrine of "*effectual calling.*" God gave to A. and B. the same call. A. obeyed the call and came to Christ, and B. refused. Now, if Paul should ask A., as he asked the Corinthian believers, "Who maketh thee to differ from another? and what hast thou that thou didst not receive?" he might answer, 'I make myself to differ from B. He had the same call that I had. He chose to reject it; I chose to accept it. I have, therefore, something which I did not receive.' And indeed upon this thing which he did not receive, his salvation depended. It is impossible that this view of the subject can produce humility so deep, or such a degree of gratitude, as that which ascribes the whole work to the Holy Spirit. Only he who believes the doctrine we are defending, can adopt the Scriptural sentiment of those beautiful verses of Watts:

"Why was I made to hear thy voice,
And enter while there's room,
When thousands make a wretched choice,
And rather starve than come?
'Twas the same love that spread the feast,
That sweetly forced us in;
Else we had still refused to taste,
And perished in our sin."

This doctrine greatly exalts the grace of God, while it deeply humbles the believer, and fills his heart with inexpressible gratitude. It proclaims "Glory to God in the highest, and on earth peace and good will to men." It will swell the sweet notes in heaven, when the head-stone of the spiritual temple shall be brought forth with shoutings of "Grace, Grace unto it."

And indeed this very feature of the doctrine marks it as Divine. Examine all the errors that have ever marred the beauty and destroyed the moral power cf the Church of Christ, and you will find in them all one great characteristic feature, viz: *they diminish the guilt of man, and thus diminish their indebtedness to divine grace.* But this doctrine humbles man in the very dust, as deserving of eternal misery, and exalts in the highest degree "the grace of God that bringeth salvation." Its language is:—"Not unto us, O Lord, not unto us, but unto thy name give glory, for thy mercy, and for thy truth's sake."* Human nature has ever exalted itself, but this doctrine humbles human nature and exalts the grace of God. It takes from man all merit, and gives all the glory of his salvation to God. Need we better evidence that this doctrine is not of man, but of God?

Nor is it wonderful, we may remark, that the doctrine of Divine foreordination has never been associated with fundamental error, and that the first step of those who wander from the cross, is the abandonment of it. Nor is it strange, that the further they wander from the truth, the more malignant their opposition to it. If man is in the condition it represents him, none but a Divine Saviour can deliver him, and a vicarious atonement is absolutely necessary to his deliverance. Such being the condition of man, the special influence of the Holy Spirit is absolutely necessary to his sanctification; and without such influence, there could be no such thing as "*effectual calling.*" While, therefore, this doctrine promotes the deepest humility and fills the heart with gratitude, it binds the soul to the Cross of Christ and suffers it not to reject any one of the great doctrines of the cross.

---

* Ps. 115: 1.

4. This doctrine secures the final perseverance of the saints. By the perseverance of the saints, we do not mean, as we are strangely misrepresented, that Christians, who are God's elect, will be saved even though they turn and commit iniquity. On the contrary, we hold that they will not turn and commit iniquity, but will *persevere* in the service of God. Or, in the beautiful language of Job:—"The righteous also shall hold on his way, and he that hath clean hands shall be stronger and stronger."* We do not assert, that the righteous never *backslide*, or become cold in the service of God, but only that they never *apostatize*. As God says of the seed of Christ: — "If his children forsake my law, and walk not in my judgments; if they break my statutes, and keep not my commandments; then will I visit their transgression with the rod, and their iniquity with stripes. Nevertheless, my loving-kindness will I not utterly take from him, nor suffer my faithfulness to fail."† God the Father has made a covenant with the Son, in which he promised that he should see of the travail of his soul and be satisfied. Now if his children prove unfaithful and backslide, he will by chastisements bring them back to the path of duty, and thus will not suffer his promise to the Son to fail. Nor do we believe, that the saints will persevere *in their own strength;* but with Paul we are "confident of this very thing, that he which hath begun a good work in them, will perform it until the day of Jesus Christ."‡ We believe that he hath given unto them eternal life, "and they shall never perish, neither shall any pluck them out

* Ch. 17: 9. † Ps 89: 30–33. ‡ Phil. 1: 6.

of his hand;" that the Father who gave them to Christ, is greater than all, and no man is able to pluck them out of his hand.*

This soul-cheering doctrine is confirmed by the doctrine of Divine foreordination. Before the foundation of the world God purposed to save his people through Christ, and he appointed and arranged all the means necessary to this end. In fulfillment of this purpose God has called them into his kingdom, and is now carrying forward his work of grace. And as Paul conclusively argues:—"If when we were enemies, we were reconciled to God by the death of his Son, much more, being reconciled, we shall be saved by his life."† That is, if, when we were in an unconverted state and full of enmity to God, he, in fulfilment of his eternal purpose, brought us into a state of reconciliation; much more, now that we are reconciled and have become his children, will he finish the work he has begun. Paul knew that all things work together for good to the people of God, because they are "*the called according to his purpose.*" He foreknew, predestined, called and justified them; and certainly he will glorify them.

These two doctrines have rarely been separated in any creed, and none who believe the doctrine of Divine foreordination, doubt the truth of the doctrine of the saints' perseverance.

5. The doctrine of Divine foreordination offers the greatest encouragement to efforts to build up the Church of Christ in the world. Men are totally depraved. Their hearts are fully set in them to do evil. Such is their love of sin, such their pride, such their enmity to

* John 10: 28, 29. † Rom. 5: 10.

God, that all the motives presented in the gospel, however eloquently set forth, fail to win them to Christ. "Paul planteth: Apollos watereth;" but unless God give the increase, their labors are in vain. But if the doctrine of Divine foreordination is true, then God can effectually call men into his kingdom; and he has purposed to renew and save a multitude that no man can number. Christians and Christian ministers feel that their success in building up the Kingdom of Christ, depends not upon sinful men, but upon the effectual working of divine grace. They can pray in faith, "Thy kingdom come;" for God has purposed that it shall come. "But as truly as I live, all the earth shall be filled with the glory of the Lord."* Daniel was encouraged to pray for the return of the Jews from the Babylonish captivity, when he "understood by books the number of the years whereof the word of the Lord came to Jeremiah the prophet, that he would accomplish seventy years in the desolation of Jerusalem."† Paul was greatly encouraged to preach the gospel in Corinth, when the Lord said to him:—"Be not afraid, but speak, and hold not thy peace; for I am with thee, and no man shall set on thee to hurt thee: for I have much people in this city."‡ And the faithful ministers of Christ, in all ages, have been cheered in their difficult work, by the assurance that God has a great multitude of people in the world, and that all whom he has given to Christ, will come to him.

Does any one ask why we pray and labor for results which are decreed of God? Why, we ask, did Daniel the prophet earnestly pray with fasting for the restora-

---

* Num. 14: 21. † Dan. 9: 1–3. ‡ Acts 18: 9, 10.

tion of the Jews, when Jeremiah had long before declared the purpose of God to restore them at the expiration of the seventy years? And why should Christians pray and labor for the conversion of the world, since God has declared his purpose to fill the world with his glory? The truth is, our prayers are not designed to change the purposes of God, nor to induce him to form new purposes neither are our labors designed to bring to pass events God has not purposed. God has appointed both *ends* and *means*, and it is the duty and the wisdom of his people to employ the means and confidently anticipate the results.

The doctrine of Divine foreordination may be misrepresented, and it may be abused; and so may the doctrine of Justification by Grace. But they who misrepresent and abuse it, are accountable for their conduct. The Christian, when he rightly understands it, will rejoice in it. All men are by nature opposed to the gospel; and if all were left to themselves, none would be saved. All who have been or who will be saved, owe their salvation to the purpose of God to bring them under the means of grace and to renew and sanctify their hearts; and they who are lost, will owe their ruin to *their sin.* Left to their choice, they rejected the gospel and lived in sin. They, therefore, will have no excuse to offer, and no charge to allege against the Divine conduct. This doctrine saves all that are saved, and injures none. It takes multitudes to heaven who would have perished; while those who are lost, perish on account of their sin.

THE END.

www.ingramcontent.com/pod-product-compliance
Lightning Source LLC
LaVergne TN
LVHW021358110826
845150LV00007B/1697

9781425513054